TWENTIETH CENTURY INTERPRETATIONS
OF

ANTONY AND CLEOPATRA

TWENTIETH CENTURY INTERPRETATIONS
OF

ANTONY AND CLEOPATRA

A Collection of Critical Essays

Edited by
MARK ROSE

Prentice-Hall, Inc. *Englewood Cliffs, N.J.*
A SPECTRUM BOOK

Library of Congress Cataloging in Publication Data
Main entry under title:

Twentieth century interpretations of Antony and Cleo-
    patra.

    (Twentieth century interpretations)   (A Spectrum
Book)
    Bibliography: p.
    1. Shakespeare, William, 1564-1616.   Antony and Cleo-
patra.   I. Rose, Mark.
PR2802.T85   822.3'3   76-47041
ISBN 0-13-038612-X
ISBN 0-13-038604-9 pbk.

To Patricia

10 9 8 7 6 5 4 3 2 1

PRENTICE-HALL INTERNATIONAL, INC., *London*
PRENTICE-HALL OF AUSTRALIA PTY. LIMITED, *Sydney*
PRENTICE-HALL OF CANADA, LTD., *Toronto*
PRENTICE-HALL OF INDIA PRIVATE LIMITED, *New Delhi*
PRENTICE-HALL OF JAPAN, INC., *Tokyo*
PRENTICE-HALL OF SOUTHEAST ASIA PTE. LTD., *Singapore*
WHITEHALL BOOKS LIMITED, *Wellington, New Zealand*

Contents

Introduction

by Mark Rose

Antony and Cleopatra occupies a rather special position in the Shakespearean canon. Probably written around 1607, some two years after Shakespeare completed the series of four great tragedies that begins with *Hamlet* and concludes with *Macbeth,* it is obviously different from them in tone and mood, and critics of the play sometimes speak of a "loosening of the tragic tension." Certainly the grand and gentle finale, Cleopatra's suicide as, royally attired in robe and crown, she takes her "baby" to her breast, is quite unlike the brutal finales of the earlier plays. If the "great" tragedies end with Aristotelian pity and fear, *Antony and Cleopatra* ends, we might almost say, with a sense of fulfillment. It would be overstating matters to assert bluntly that at the conclusion Antony and Cleopatra are married in death. Yet I do not think we can avoid feeling some satisfaction, perhaps even some joy, when Cleopatra says, "Husband, I come." In *Antony and Cleopatra* Shakespeare appears to be moving a little way toward the late romances—*Cymbeline, The Winter's Tale,* and *The Tempest*—those bittersweet plays in which love at last triumphs and things lost are miraculously recovered.

In structure, too, *Antony and Cleopatra* is quite unlike the earlier tragedies. Especially in *Hamlet, Othello,* and *Lear,* Shakespeare tends to organize his material into a relatively few, massively built scenes. In *Antony and Cleopatra,* however, he multiplies short scenes at a dizzying rate, leaping about the Mediterranean world from Egypt to Rome to Messina in Sicily and even to Syria. To a reader or audience more familiar with the technique of the earlier tragedies, *Antony and Cleopatra* may seem confusing, and we may be tempted, as Samuel Johnson evidently was when he condemned the play as merely a string of episodes "produced without any art of connection or care of disposition," to suppose that Shakespeare never achieved complete control over his story.

Despite the complex surface, however, the underlying narrative pattern is simple. In the first half of the play Antony detaches himself from Cleopatra and travels to Rome, where he makes peace with Octavius Caesar, confirming their accord by marrying Caesar's sister. The play's second half finds Antony reunited with Cleopatra, and in this movement Caesar travels from Rome to Egypt and demolishes the lovers' world.

Even more important than the narrative pattern in the play's structure is the thematic contrast between Caesar's stern Rome and Cleopatra's luxurious Egypt. More than locales, Rome and Egypt—the one associated with prudence, discipline, and conquest; the other with fertility, pleasure, and love—represent opposed philosophies, opposed perspectives on life, or as Northrop Frye puts it in "The Tailors of the Earth," the one suggests "the day world of history," the other "the night world of passion." In no other tragedy does Shakespeare establish quite so bold a thematic opposition, and it is this opposition that allows him to exercise extraordinary freedom in other aspects of dramatic organization.

One function of the play's apparent looseness, its short scenes and sprawling geography, is to create an epic effect appropriate to this tragedy on a classical subject. Shakespeare's principal source for the lovers' story was Plutarch's *Life of Antony* in North's translation, but in shaping his play he drew upon a wide range of medieval and Renaissance literature. Hardly less important than Plutarch is the tradition of the Renaissance epic poem— Ariosto's *Orlando Furioso,* Tasso's *Jerusalem Delivered,* Spenser's *Faerie Queene*—with its dual focus on love and war and its recurring figure of the great hero torn between his love for a beautiful enchantress and the claims of glory, duty, and the battlefield. When Antony insists that he must break off from his "enchanting" queen, we can hear echoes of a series of famous protagonists, going back at least as far as Vergil's Aeneas, constrained by fate to abandon Dido in order to found Rome. Of course, unlike his literary ancestors, Antony never does quite break his Egyptian fetters, and in this fact we can find an important clue to the way Shakespeare has translated an epic formula into tragedy.

In the epics there is little question of what is proper for the protagonist to do: he must fulfill his heroic destiny. Often the decision to be made is a fairly straightforward choice between

good and evil. Cleopatra's magical charms may recall the more
sinister charms of the witches of the epics, but she is only meta-
phorically an enchantress and by no means evil. In the play it is
only the Romans—and Antony in his Roman moods—who see
things in epic terms, disdaining love as dotage. Philo introduces
this point of view when he complains about the change in Antony
since he has been in Egypt:

>   Those his goodly eyes
> That o'er the files and musters of the war
> Have glowed like plated Mars, now bend, now turn
> The office and devotion of their view
> Upon a tawny front.   (I.i.2-6)

And yet, despite the Romans' persistent evocation of the epic
values, the play compels us to see that Octavius' Rome is somewhat less than heroic. Indeed, the image of Rome comes in for
some hard satirical knocks—in the drunken scene on Pompey's
galley, for example, or in the brief scene in Syria in which Ventidius explains that it is imprudent for a lieutenant to make too
great a name for himself in his captain's absence. What Shakespeare has done is to lift the epic point of view out of its original
context and make it dramatic.

The lovers' language asserts an alternative point of view that
recalls a very different literary tradition—the Tudor morality
plays. As scholars have more and more begun to recognize, the
popular drama of Renaissance England is a direct descendant of
the vigorous tradition of the moralities, and in nearly all his
tragedies Shakespeare draws in some fashion upon the formulas
of these plays. The recurring figure of the moralities is of course
Everyman—or Mankind or Humanus Genus—torn between the
temptations of the world and the rewards of eternity. In a strik-
ingly similar fashion, Antony is torn between his desire for
worldly power and his love for a queen who insists that it is
"paltry to be Caesar." Repeatedly, the lovers assert that there is
something transcendent about their passion, as when Cleopatra
reminds Antony that

> Eternity was in our lips and eyes,
> Bliss in our brows' bent: none our parts so poor
> But was a race of heaven.   (I.iii.35-37)

From this point of view kingdoms are clay and the world a snare

to trap an aspiring spirit. The vision is compelling, and yet the
spiritual values that the lovers evoke are not wholly appropriate
to their situation, for these are ultimately the Christian values
of *contemptus mundi* literature, and Antony and Cleopatra,
voluptuous and full-blooded, are neither Christians nor in any
Christian sense unworldly. Again, Shakespeare has inserted a
point of view into an alien context and made it dramatic.

The two patterns that lie behind *Antony and Cleopatra*, the
epic formula and the morality formula, are fundamentally in-
compatible. In the one, Cleopatra is a dangerous enchantress
and Antony wastes himself in yielding to her charms. In the
other, she is the magical embodiment of something with which
the claims of Caesar and Empire cannot compare. Moreover,
although each formula has a degree of validity, neither is wholly
convincing in the context of the play and thus neither can cancel
the other and assert its own values as a kind of final truth.

Perhaps students sometimes find *Antony and Cleopatra* baffling
precisely because, unlike *Hamlet, Othello, Lear,* and *Macbeth,*
this play provides no final "truth," no moral point of reference
from which the action may be judged. The earlier tragedies all
have prominent villains—Claudius, Iago, Goneril and Regan,
Macbeth—and each to some degree depends for its effect upon
arousing the audience's horrified fascination with evil at work.
Antony and Cleopatra is not concerned with evil. Octavius, for
example, may be as ambitious as Claudius or Macbeth, but the
play never requires us to regard even his most cold-blooded actions as criminal. There are no villains here and horror is no
part of the play's effect.

Plays that do arouse horror generally engage the audience's
emotions directly in the action. The earlier tragedies achieve
this direct engagement to a remarkable degree. *Antony and Cleopatra* places us more at a distance. We do not partake of the
tragedy so much as observe it as a spectacle. It is notable, for
instance, that none of the three principal characters—Antony,
Cleopatra, or Caesar—has a major soliloquy. We view them
almost entirely from the outside and generally in more or less
public circumstances. Indeed, the play is often explicitly spectacular. The opening scene in which the lovers cross the stage
accompanied by eunuchs and attendants is a kind of public
procession. Enobarbus describes Cleopatra's fabulous aquatic

pageant on Cydnus, and Caesar describes the spectacle of the lovers enthroned in the marketplace of Alexandria. Even the finale, the scene that comes closest to evoking sustained emotional engagement, is spectacular in spirit, a formal show of royalty in death.

The play's characteristic distancing of the audience manifests itself also in poetic style. There are two readily distinguishable poetic styles, one associated with Rome, the other with Egypt. The Roman style, which has affinities with the marmoreal verse of *Julius Caesar,* is emphatic, relatively free of metaphor, and seems almost designed to hide rather than reveal deep emotion. Caesar's first speech provides a good example of its tone:

> You may see, Lepidus, and henceforth know
> It is not Caesar's natural vice to hate
> Our great competitor. From Alexandria
> This is the news: he fishes, drinks, and wastes
> The lamps of night in revel; is not more manlike
> Than Cleopatra, nor the queen of Ptolemy
> More womanly than he; hardly gave audience, or
> Vouchsafed to think he had partners. You shall find there
> A man who is the abstract of all faults
> That all men follow. (I.iv.1-10)

There is little sense here of a mind at work: the thought seems prefabricated, conceived in advance. The contrasting Egyptian style is much more dramatically exciting than the Roman, but in terms of sincerity of emotion it is equally impenetrable. Compare, for example, Antony's hyperbolic verse with Hamlet's knotty, passionate punning or with Macbeth's scaring imagery:

> Let Rome in Tiber melt and the wide arch
> Of the ranged empire fall! Here is my space.
> Kingdoms are clay: our dungy earth alike
> Feeds beast as man. The nobleness of life
> Is to do thus, when such a mutual pair
> And such a twain can do't, in which I bind,
> On pain of punishment, the world to weet
> We stand up peerless. (I.i.33-40)

Caesar is cool and remote, Antony in his Egyptian mood is declamatory and theatrical, but both the Roman and the Egyptian are essentially public styles.

The public and spectacular quality of *Antony and Cleopatra* is perhaps best understood in connection with its classical subject, for, unlike the four major tragedies that precede it, this play is essentially a historical drama. In *Antony and Cleopatra* Shakespeare is dramatizing what for his audience was one of the best-known stories in history—Caesar says of the dead lovers that "No grave upon the earth shall clip in it/A pair so famous" (V.ii.357-358)—and this fact is crucial to an appreciation of the kind of effect he is trying to achieve. The past in this play remains the past, multicolored and fascinating, but always at a certain distance. Most important, history passes before us as a pageant moving toward an end known in advance. The preceding tragedies provide us with moral vantage points; the final "truth" in *Antony and Cleopatra,* the secure vantage point from which we view the action, is simply our knowledge of how the story came out.

Shakespeare never allows us to forget that the destinies of these famous men and women are fixed and unchangeable. The soothsayer, appearing in the second scene, contributes from the start a sense not so much of doom—for the play is not brooding or gloomy—but of inevitability, and later in Rome he reappears to inform Antony of what we in the audience know to be truth: Caesar's fortunes will rise higher than Antony's. In the first half of the seventh scene, II.ii, Antony arranges to marry Octavia, but the scene's second half comments ironically on the event when Enobarbus declares that Antony will never abandon Cleopatra, and this prophecy, too, reminds us of our historical distance from the action because we know that Enobarbus is correct.

For us the play is fixed in history, but for the characters the future is fluid with possibility. One of the particular triumphs of *Antony and Cleopatra* is the success with which it manages to convey both these points of view at once, showing us the completed past in the process of becoming. So far from being rigid, the world of the play, as Maynard Mack among others emphasizes, is pre-eminently a world in rapid motion, a liquid world, characterized by images of rivers flooding, things melting. Indeed, the play's narrative pattern, the movement from Egypt to Rome and back to Egypt again, has something of a tidal rhythm about it, so that one may think of Caesar's image of the "vagabond flag" that "Goes to and back, lackeying the varying tide,/ To rot itself with motion" (I.iv.45-47). The brevity of the scenes, the extraordinary number of exits and entrances, the messengers hurrying across vast distances, all these contribute to a sense of a rushing, unstable world.

It is a world in which information is often dated or inaccurate and in which action must be based upon uncertain knowledge. In the fourth scene Caesar deplores Antony's continuing revels, but we know that Antony is already on his way to Rome. Cleopatra is furious at the news of Antony's marriage, but in fact he has already decided to return to her. We hear a great deal, too, about the uncertainty of human wishes, the instability of desire. Cleopatra understands fickleness well and knows she is in continual danger of losing Antony's affections. Antony, surprised by his own feelings when he learns of Fulvia's death, appears to regard fickleness as one of the elemental laws of life:

> Thus did I desire it:
> What our contempts doth often hurl from us,
> We wish it ours again. The present pleasure,
> By revolution low'ring, does become
> The opposite of itself: she's good, being gone.
> (I,ii.118-122)

Later in the same scene Antony speaks of "Our slippery people,/ Whose love is never linked to the deserver/ Till his deserts are past" (181-183), and Caesar expresses similar sentiments in the fourth scene. After Antony's death, Agrippa, seeing Caesar's tears, comments on the strangeness "That nature must compel us to lament/ Our most persisted deeds" (V,i.29-30). History, the play seems to suggest, is made in confusion, created in the midst of uncertain information about other people and, even more to the point, in the midst of uncertain knowledge of ourselves.

The one character who evidently knows what he wants is Octavius Caesar, who moves in an unswerving course against Pompey, Lepidus, and finally, Antony. In creating Caesar, Shakespeare may have had in mind his earlier historical tragedy, *Richard II*, where he had drawn a similar portrait of political success in Henry Bolingbroke, who, like Caesar, reveals nothing about his purposes while steadily advancing upon the crown. But Caesar, if anything, is more single-minded than Bolingbroke. Shakespeare emphasizes the narrow, puritanical efficiency of this man who seems to regard any activity not directed toward political ends as worthless. Devoid of mirth himself, Caesar is consistently contemptuous of levity. One of his characteristic words is "waste," as when he speaks of Antony wasting the nights in revels or when he grudgingly accepts his army's periodic need for entertainment, commanding Maecenas to feast the soldiers: "We have store to do't,/ And they have earned the waste" (IV.i.15-16). In temperament Caesar has much in common with certain figures from Shakespeare's comedies. Malvolio and Shylock, for example, are similarly mirthless—they are, as we should say today, "compulsive personalities"—and Shylock's contempt for Christian "prodigality" is not unlike Caesar's attitude toward "waste." In the comedies such puritanical figures, being antithetical to the generosity and flexibility of spirit that these plays celebrate, are always defeated. But in *Antony and Cleopatra* Octavius is the victor. In the world of history single-mindedness and perhaps even narrowness of sympathy can be an advantage, and, while the play does not celebrate Caesar's qualities, it does not condemn them.

Antony, as great a lover of pleasure as he is of power, is at the opposite extreme of human nature from Caesar. In the root sense of the word he is "magnanimous," large of spirit. When Enobarbus deserts him Antony is sympathetic rather than vengeful: "O, my fortunes have/ Corrupted honest men!" (IV.v.16-17) he exclaims, and orders Enobarbus' treasure sent to him. Antony is what Enobarbus calls him, a mine of bounty, and everything he does— loving, feasting, fighting—he does bounteously, with energy and spirit. Significantly, it is Antony, not Caesar, who is described as glowing like Mars in battle. Whereas Caesar is a manipulator, Antony is a warrior and he seeks to immerse himself in the world rather than to control it from a distance. But the very qualities that make Antony appealing make him vulnerable to Caesar's calculations. At Actium, the great turning-point in the history the play relates, Antony characteristically disdains to fight by land precisely because by land his superiority is certain and Caesar dares him to fight by sea. Prudent in all things, Caesar never takes unnecessary risks. But Antony, like so many of Shakespeare's comic protagonists, chooses to entrust himself to fortune—frequently an emblem of fortune, the sea here is also associated with Cleopatra and the Egyptian way of doing things—and the gesture in the context of this play is as foolish as it is admirable.

Sometimes in a Shakespearean play a common word will become especially charged with meanings, gathering together many of the play's key concerns. In *Hamlet* "act" is such a word, reaching out to include both the idea of taking action and that of playing a role, of acting. In *Antony and Cleopatra* the word "becomes" appears with unusual frequency; in fact it is used more often here than in any play of Shakespeare's except *The Winter's Tale,* which is also concerned with process, with becoming. In *Antony and Cleopatra,* however, "becomes" is most often employed in connection with the idea of decorum in the sense of something being a fitting and proper adornment. Thus Antony speaks of Cleopatra as a "wrangling queen" whom "every thing becomes" (I.i.48-49). When Antony is angry, Cleopatra asks Charmian to observe "How this Herculean Roman does become/ The carriage of his chafe" (I.iii.84-85). And Enobarbus, praising Cleopatra to the Romans, says that

> vilest things
> Become themselves in her, that the holy priests
> Bless her when she is riggish.   (II.ii.239-241)

Things "become themselves" in her. This rather tangled phrase conveys the notion of these qualities, paradoxically, being in Cleopatra an adornment, but it also suggests things "becoming themselves" in the sense of being at last realized, brought to fulfillment.

The play is concerned with "becoming" in all these senses, and it is also concerned with the idea of selfhood, of individuality brought to fulfillment. Antony and Cleopatra insist upon their own greatness and uniqueness, and the play keeps the concern with selfhood before us in such phrases as Cleopatra's "Antony/ Will be himself" (I.i.42-43), Philo's reference to times when Antony is "not Antony" (I.i.57), or Enobarbus' statement that in the meeting with Caesar he will entreat Antony to "answer like himself" (II.ii.4). Antony's comic description of the crocodile— "It is shaped, sir, like itself" (II.vii.41)—is a burlesque upon the same theme. Process and change, growth toward fulfillment, fitness, decorum, and selfhood—these concepts are very closely associated in *Antony and Cleopatra.* After Actium, as the future gradually becomes apparent even to those within history, the issue becomes less a question of destiny, of whether Antony or Caesar will triumph, than one of identity—that is, will Antony and Cleopatra prove true or false to themselves? Will they, in the several senses of the word, "become" themselves in their ends?

   The issue emerges from a context in which the question of
fidelity to others is frequently raised, as, for instance, when
Cleopatra receives Thidias with a courtesy that suggests she may
be considering deserting Antony, or when the Egyptian sailors
in the second naval battle cast up their caps and join ranks with
Caesar's. Has Cleopatra betrayed Antony, sold him to Caesar as
he first believes, or have her sailors betrayed her? These questions
remain unanswered, becoming lost as the play progresses in the
more basic issue of fidelity to oneself, which Enobarbus' death
brings into focus. Superficially a pragmatist, Enobarbus decides
that Antony's cause is hopeless and abandons him only to discover
that in leaving his master he has betrayed his own nobler self.
Broken-hearted with shame at his own baseness, Enobarbus simply disintegrates and dies.
   Not good or evil, but nobility or baseness—these have all along
been the terms in which the play's basic issues are formulated. Is
greatness to be found in pursuit of empire or, as Antony pro-
claims in the first scene, is the nobility of life only discoverable in
a different kind of space? Which is freedom, which subjection,
the public life of Rome or the life of pleasure in Egypt? The issues
of the earlier part of the play admit no possibility of solution,
but toward the end, when the general shape of destiny is fixed,
the choices become clearer. Faced with degradation in Rome or
suicide, Antony remains faithful to himself, and from no point of
view that the play provides can his death be seen as ignoble:

> The miserable change now at my end
> Lament nor sorrow at; but please your thoughts
> In feeding them with those my former fortunes,
> Wherein I lived the greatest prince o'th'world,
> The noblest: and do not now basely die,
> Not cowardly put off my helmet to
> My countryman. A Roman, by a Roman
> Valiantly vanquished.   (IV.xv.51-58)

Earlier Antony was torn between Cleopatra and the claims of
empire; now there is no choice to be made and he dies embracing
his destiny, laying, like an offering, a final kiss upon Cleopatra's
lips.
   After Antony's death our attention is wholly upon Cleopatra,
and in the long finale—at over 350 lines the concluding scene is
by far the play's longest—the rush of events ceases and the play

builds to a full orchestral close. For Cleopatra as for Antony the issue is less whether she will be faithful to her lover than whether she will be faithful to herself. Once again the issue is formulated as a choice between nobility and baseness, but it is presented in a style that is all Cleopatra's.

If Shakespeare's Caesar is prudent and his Antony generous, his Cleopatra is above all an actress. Cleopatra's sense of pageantry establishes much of what I have called the play's spectacular quality. She is always, it seems, dressing up in costume, presenting herself theatrically as Venus on Cydnus or as Isis in Alexandria. With Antony himself she is no less the actress, taking her cue from his moods but not in an obvious or amaturish manner:

> See where he is, who's with him, what he does:
> I did not send you. If you find him sad,
> Say I am dancing; if in mirth, report
> That I am sudden sick.   (I.iii.2-5)

Cleopatra is hardly the idle queen the Romans imagine. Sometimes she presents herself as idle, but it is a role constructed, as she tells Antony, with "sweating labor" (I.iii.93). The only time Cleopatra is actually idle is when Antony is absent and she is without an audience. Aware of herself as a player of roles, Cleopatra is able to puncture Antony's less self-conscious posturing, as in the opening scene when she exclaims "Excellent falsehood!" (I.i.40) in response to his declaration of love or when she teases him into anger as he is taking his solemn leave of her in the third scene:

> Good now, play one scene
> Of excellent dissembling, and let it look,
> Like perfect honor.   (I.iii.78-80)

Paradoxically, at such moments Cleopatra, who is admittedly acting, seems more sincere than Antony; but, finally, the very concept of sincerity seems inappropriate in connection with her, for in all things and at all times, whether playing to an audience of one such as Antony or Thidias or to all Alexandria, she is an artist.

After Antony's death, Cleopatra, characteristically, sees herself as facing a theatrical choice. Will she allow Caesar to make an ignoble show of her in Rome, parading her through the streets for "mechanic slaves" to ogle?

> Saucy lictors
> Will catch at us like strumpets, and scald rhymers
> Ballad us out o' tune. The quick comedians
> Extemporally will stage us, and present
> Our Alexandrian revels: Antony
> Shall be brought drunken forth, and I shall see
> Some squeaking Cleopatra boy my greatness
> I'th' posture of a whore.   (V.ii.214-221)

The play's last contest, the battle of wits between Caesar and Cleo-patra, is essentially a struggle over who will stage the Egyptian queen's final show. Moreover, the struggle itself is theatrical, a contest of feigning, for Caesar must present himself as well-mean-ing whereas Cleopatra must assume the role of fearful woman. Caesar may be the world's master but in this kind of contest he is no match for Cleopatra, who sees through his display of gener-osity—"He words me, girls, he words me, that I should not/ Be noble to myself!" (V.ii.191-192)—at the same time as she succeeds in deceiving him about her purposes.

Perhaps because she is conscious of herself as a player of roles, Cleopatra is also aware of her common humanity. When Iras rouses her from her grief at Antony's death by calling "Royal Egypt! Empress!" (IV.xv.74), Cleopatra denies her titles:

> No more but e'en a woman, and commanded
> By such poor passion as the maid that milks
> And does the meanest chares.   (IV.xv.76-78)

And yet even the poorest instrument, as she remarks about the fig peddler, may do a noble deed. In her last pageant, Cleopatra, calling for her robe and crown, presents herself to eternity as a queen and Antony's wife, creating a formal tableau of royalty in death. What she terms her "noble act" (V.ii.284)—"act" has the same double meaning here as in *Hamlet*—represents her triumph over not only Caesar but over mutability, over inconstancy of desire and all the fickle, uncertain processes of nature.

Cleopatra's triumph is peculiarly her own. An artist whose medium has always been her own person, she conquers mut-ability, mere "fortune," by transforming herself into a work of art, fixed for all time. Shakespeare makes much toward the end of Cleopatra's "monument"—after Antony's death the monument is, the anonymous Egyptian messenger tells Caesar, "all she has" (V.i.53)—and, significantly too, Cleopatra speaks of herself at the end as no longer flesh and blood but "marble-constant" (V.ii.240) from head to foot. If in *Antony and Cleopatra* Shakespeare appears to be moving a little way toward the mood and concerns of the late romances, we may now note that the play's conclusion curiously foreshadows that of *The Winter's Tale*. There Hermione's statue miraculously comes alive, leaving the frozen world of art and entering nature. Here Cleopatra in effect becomes a statue, her own enduring monument. In both plays the dominant note struck at the end is one of wonder at a marvel in which nature and art interpenetrate. But *Antony and Cleopatra* differs from *The Winter's Tale* in a great many ways and not least in that whereas the later play is a "tale" and the outcome is surprising, *Antony and Cleopatra* is history with the conclusion known in advance. The tragedy leaves us with a special feeling of fulfillment, for what we witness at end is the spectacle of life becoming history, of Antony and Cleopatra at last becoming "themselves" as we who have observed their lives across a great gap of time have always known them to be.

PART ONE
Backgrounds

Style in the Roman Plays

by Maurice Charney

Although the Roman plays have some strong similarities as a group—their use of "Roman" costume, their favorable Roman idea of suicide, their common source in Plutarch—they are stylistically quite different. The strongest contrast is between the styles of *Julius Caesar* and *Antony and Cleopatra*, which I should like to consider before going on to discuss *Coriolanus*. Actually, the Roman world in *Antony and Cleopatra* is very much like that in *Julius Caesar*, but it is "overreached" by the world of Empire and the splendors and perils of Egypt. Antony abandons the Roman style and values of Octavius Caesar—they are public, political, and objective as in *Julius Caesar*—and enters into the Egyptian style and values of Cleopatra. These two plays show the working of Shakespeare's imagination in two different moods: in *Julius Caesar* he seems to be deliberately limiting his imaginative resources, while in *Antony and Cleopatra* he appears to be trying to extend them "past the size of dreaming."...

The characteristic figure in *Antony and Cleopatra* is the hyperbole, or what Puttenham in his *Arte of English Poesie* (1589) calls "for his immoderate excesse...the ouer reacher" or "the loud lyer,"[1] and he defines it as "by incredible comparison giuing credit."[2] In Greek "hyperbole" is *a throwing beyond: an over-*

"Style in the Roman Plays." From *Shakespeare's Roman Plays: The Function of Imagery in the Drama,* by Maurice Charney (Cambridge, Mass.: Harvard University Press, 1961), pp. 11, 2-27. Reprinted, with alteration of the original footnote numbering by permission of the author and publishers. Copyright © 1961 by the President and Fellows of Harvard College. A discussion of the style of *Julius Caesar* is omitted here.

[1]George Puttenham, *The Arte of English Poesie,* ed. Gladys Doidge Willcock and Alice Walker, Cambridge, 1936, p. 191.

[2]*Ibid.,* p. 154. Compare Harry Levin's comment on Marlowe's dramatic use of hyperbole: "The stage becomes a vehicle for hyperbole, not merely by accredit-

15

shooting, superiority, excess in anything…" (Lidell-Scott Dictionary). It would include the ideas of extravagance and boldness as well as exaggeration and overstatement. In essence, hyperbole is the reaching-out of the imagination for superlatives. This is I think what Coleridge means when he calls the style of *Antony and Cleopatra "feliciter audax"*—literally, "felicitously bold or audacious," but perhaps best rendered by Coleridge's phrase. "happy valiancy of style."[3]

This type of style is demanded by the spaciousness and scope of the play's themes. Perhaps the best example is Cleopatra's dream of Antony:

> His face was as the heav'ns, and therein stuck
> A sun and moon, which kept their course and lighted
> The little O, the earth.   (5.2.79-81)

The image of Antony becomes the whole cosmos, and this earth is only a "little O" in comparison—we cannot imagine in higher terms. Cleopatra continues: "His legs bestrid the ocean: his rear'd arm/ Crested the world" (5.2.82-83). This is the Marlovian strain of invidious comparison in which man is literally made the measure of all things. Cleopatra goes so far as to question the reality of her dream, as if it were beyond our mortal sense of possibility:

> Think you there was or might be such a man
> As this I dreamt of?
> *Dol.*   Gentle madam, no.
> *Cleo.* You lie, up to the hearing of the gods!
>   But, if there be or ever were one such,
>   It's past the size of dreaming. Nature wants stuff
>   To vie strange forms with fancy; yet, t'imagine
>   An Antony were nature's piece 'gainst fancy,
>   Condemning shadows quite.   (5.2.93-100)

ing the incredible or supporting rhetoric with a platform and sounding board, but by taking metaphors literally and acting concepts out. Operating visually as well as vocally, it converts symbols into properties; triumph must ride across in a chariot, hell must flare up in fire works; students, no longer satisfied to read about Helen of Troy, must behold her in her habit as she lived. Whereas poetry is said to transport us to an imaginative level, poetic drama transports that level to us; hyperbolically speaking, it brings the mountain to Mohammed" (*The Overreacher: A Study of Christopher Marlowe,* Cambridge, Mass., 1952, p. 24).

[3]*Coleridge's Shakespearean Criticism,* ed. Thomas Middleton Raysor, London, 1930, I, 86.

The image of Antony is "past the size of dreaming." It is un-realizable because reality ("Nature") cannot present all the forms imagination ("fancy," a kind of dreaming) can conceive. But even to think that the forms of imagination may actually exist is an argument for "Nature." We may take this statement—"Nature wants stuff/ To vie strange forms with fancy"—as a key to the character of the style. The imagination acts as hyperbole: it throws beyond, overshoots, is superior to, and in excess of nature, yet it cannot go past the size of dreaming, and therefore must remain implicit in the dramatic action and words. Where *Julius Caesar* limits and defines its figures and insists on the proper logical application of vehicle to tenor, *Antony and Cleopatra* uses a figurative language, the "strange forms" of "fancy," that tries to force itself beyond the bounds of mere "Nature."

The "hyperbolical" quality of *Antony and Cleopatra* is also seen in a special kind of superlative. When Antony tells Cleo-patra, "Now for the love of Love and her soft hours..." (1.1.44), the doubling of the noun with "of" serves as an intensifier: it is an attempt to get at the quintessence. Antony is Cleopatra's "man of men" (1.5.72), as if only he among men could represent Man. He is also her "Lord of lords!" (4.8.16), and his sons are proclaimed "kings of kings" (3.6.13). This grammatical form echoes in the mind when we hear Antony say that Cleopatra

> Like a right gypsy hath at fast and loose
> Beguil'd me to the very heart of loss!
> (4.12.28-29)

No loss can be imagined greater; it is an absolute, the essence and the life of loss.

The range of diction in *Antony and Cleopatra* is very wide, and it shows an extravagant juxtaposing of latinate and colloquial words, as in Cleopatra's speech to the asp:

> Come, thou mortal wretch,
> With thy sharp teeth this knot intrinsicate
> Of life at once untie. Poor venomous fool,
> Be angry, and dispatch. (5.2.306-309)

"Intrinsicate" was considered a pedantic, "inkhorn" term in its time, a fit object for satire in Marston's *The Scourge of Villanie* (1599). When his poem "shall come into the late perfumed fist of iudiciall *Torquatus*...he will vouchsafe it, some of his new-minted Epithets, (as *Reall, Intrinsecate, Delphicke,*)....."[4] "Intrinsicate" was often used for "intricate" and meant much the same thing: "involved," "complicated," "entangled." But it also suggests a connection with "intrinsic," which refers to the essential nature of a thing. Life is the intrinsic knot—intricate, entangled, essential—which the asp, as death the lover, will at once untie. Alongside this uncommon word, "intrinsicate," are such familiar terms of endearment as "mortal wretch" and "Poor venomous fool." The use of the colloquial in Cleopatra's speech to the asp appeals to the common human emotions of tragedy, while the latinate has a heightening effect. Charmian's words on the death of her mistress also illustrate this two-fold quality:

> Now boast thee, death, in thy possession lies
> A lass unparallel'd. Downy windows, close;
> And golden Phoebus never be beheld
> Of eyes again so royal!   (5.2.318-21)

The homely and familiar "lass" is placed between the long latinate words "possession" and "unparallel'd." It recalls the Cleopatra of

> No more but e'en a woman, and commanded
> By such poor passion as the maid that milks
> And does the meanest chares.   (4.15.73-75)

The effect of "lass"—a common, lowly word—is immediately countered by the periphrasis of "Downy windows" for eyes and the mythological reference to "golden Phoebus."[5] The verbal

---

[4] John Marston, Preface to *The Scourge of Villanie* (1599), ed. G. B. Harrison, London, 1925, p. 9. See I. A. Richards' comment on "intrinsicate" in *The Philosophy of Rhetoric*, N. Y., 1936, pp. 64-65.

[5] See John Middleton Murry, *Shakespeare*, N.Y., 1936, p. 298. Another example, very obvious and powerful, of this double effect is in Macbeth's harrowing consciousness of guilt:

> Will all great Neptune's ocean wash this blood
> Clean from my hand? No. This my hand will rather
> The multitudinous seas incarnadine,
> Making the green one red.   (2.2.60-63)

The simple "green" and "red" restate "multitudinous seas" and "incarnadine" and act as a relief to these learned words. See John Crowe Ransom, "On Shakespeare's Language," *SR*, LV (1947), 181-98.

context is further enriched by a covert allusion. Cleopatra, the "lass unparallel'd," now triumphs over Caesar, the "ass/Unpolicied" (5.2.310-11)—the half-rhyme deliberately pairs these latinate-colloquial phrases.[6]

Going beyond the effects of rhetoric, we may explore the "hyperbolical" style of *Antony and Cleopatra* in a more extended example. Cleopatra's "infinite variety"[7] is a leading hyperbole in the play, and it draws its strength as much from the poetic language lavished on Cleopatra as from the presented image of her character—the role demands an "infinite variety" of gesture and stage action. The explication of this elaborate hyperbole may serve as a parallel to the analysis of the scene of Caesar's Ghost; in both places there is a very characteristic expression of the play's style.

The ambivalent tone of "infinite variety" is first established by Enobarbus right after his splendid speech about Cleopatra in her barge on the Cydnus. He assures Maecenas that Antony cannot break off from his "enchanting queen":

> Never! He will not.
> Age cannot wither her nor custom stale
> Her infinite variety. Other woman cloy
> The appetites they feed, but she makes hungry
> Where most she satisfies; for vilest things
> Become themselves in her, that the holy priests
> Bless her when she is riggish.   (2.2.239-45)

Cleopatra is outside the withering toils of age and custom and cloying appetite, for "vilest things/ Become themselves in her," achieve their apotheosis and inner perfection. She is even blessed when she plays the strumpet ("is riggish")—this is the strange issue of the "holy palmers' kiss" of *Romeo and Juliet* (1.5.102). We have been prepared for Enobarbus' statement by many previous expressions of Cleopatra's variousness and her capacity to exploit the range of emotions. She is Antony's

> wrangling queen!
> Whom every thing becomes—to chide, to laugh,
> To weep....   (1.1.48-50)

[6]See George Rylands, "Shakespeare's Poetic Energy," *Proc. Brit. Acad.* 1951, XXXVII, 101.

[7]Peter G. Phialas notes in his New Yale Shakespeare edition (New Haven, 1955, pp. 142-43) that the phrase "infinite varietie" occurs in Florio's Montaigne (Modern Library edition, 1933, p. 108).

She knows how to manipulate her sentiments and to stimulate passion by "infinite variety." As she tells the incredulous Charmian in her message to Antony:

> If you find him sad,
> Say I am dancing; if in mirth, report
> That I am sudden sick.   (1.3.3-5)

This is beyond Charmian's comprehension, but Cleopatra is herself a "heavenly mingle" (1.5.59), and she knows the art to "make defect perfection" (2.2.236).

These paradoxical aspects of Cleopatra may be demonstrated in II,v, where her "infinite variety" is seen as roving desire searching for objects. We begin with the consciously poetic and languorous tone of *Twelfth Night:* "Give me some music! music, moody food/ Of us that trade in love" (2.5.1-2). The music is called for, and Mardian the Eunuch enters, but Cleopatra is no longer interested in hearing him sing: "Let it alone! Let's to billiards" (2.5.3). Now begins a series of sexual puns in the style of Shakespeare's early comedies; Cleopatra explores the witty possibilities of "play":

> *Cleo.* As well a woman with an eunuch play'd
>   As with a woman. Come, you'll play with me, sir?
> *Mar.* As well as I can, madam.
> *Cleo.* And when good will is show'd, though 't come too short,
>   The actor may plead pardon.   (2.5.5-9)

But she quickly tires of this verbal sport and has a new whim:

> Give me mine angle! we'll to th' river. There,
> My music playing far off, I will betray
> Tawny-finn'd fishes. My bended hook shall pierce
> Their slimy jaws; and as I draw them up,
> I'll think them every one an Antony,
> And say, "Ah, ha! y'are caught!"   (2.5.10-15)

The suggestions of music at the opening of the scene is taken up again, but the mood is entirely different. The absent Antony is "caught" or "hooked" in the physically violent image of the slimy-jawed fish, which is much transmuted from the incident in Plutarch of the salt fish attached as a jest to Antony's line.

Once struck, the note of passion is intensified with the appearance of the Messenger:

> O, from Italy!
> Ram thou thy fruitful tidings in mine ears,
> That long time have been barren.
> (2.5.23-25)

It is a sudden sexual fury to have Antony himself in the tidings about him. When the Messenger tells his news of Antony's marriage, he is struck down by Cleopatra (2.5.61 s.d., 62 s.d.), haled up and down (2.5.64 s.d.), and threatened with a knife (2.5.73 s.d.). The luxuriant poetic tone of the passage has now issued into the physical violence of the stage action. This is all part of the style of Cleopatra's "infinite variety," which runs the gamut from "music, moody food" to "Rogue, thou hast liv'd too long" with the stage direction *Draw a knife.*

In contrast to this scene we have the "infinite variety" of Cleopatra's suicide, which is not quite done in the "high Roman fashion" (4.15.87), but with a priestly deliberateness and an aesthetic enjoyment of robe and crown and the effect of the asp-bite. Shakespeare here takes advantage of all the richness of the Elizabethan staging to enforce the poetic splendor of Cleopatra's final scene. She is to be shown "like a queen" (5.2.227) in elaborate stage ritual and costume, and we know from Henslowe's account books and other sources how important gorgeous robes were to an Elizabethan production.

In her death Caesar affirms her magnificence:

> she looks like sleep,
> As she would catch another Antony
> In her strong toil of grace.
> (5.2.349-51)

Part of the effectiveness of this passage rests in the manner of portrayal. Cleopatra must really look "like sleep," with an indefinable expression of grace—perhaps a smile. In Elizabethan English "grace" is a complex word whose meanings range from physical attraction and charm of personal manner to pre-eminence of nobility, moral rightness, and divine blessing. Cleopatra's "strong toil of grace" is a union of the queen who "beggar'd all description" (2.2.203) and the "serpent of old Nile" (1.5.25)— she could "catch another Antony" now as she caught the first one. We recall Cleopatra fishing in II,v; there the hooked fish was Antony, over whom she uttered the triumphant cry, "'Ah, ha!

y'are caught!'" (2.5.15). We should not overlook the violence in
Cleopatra's "strong toil of grace" and its ability to "catch." The
word "Toil," for example, refers to a net or trap to snare game.
Although Cleopatra is heightened by her death, her character
and motives remain in a certain ambiguity even at the end. She is
always both "queen" (female monarch) and "quean" (wench,
whore), and in this covert pun[8] lies the secret of her attraction.

[8]Helge Kökeritz discusses the possibility of this pun, but regards it as "dubious." It is possible in colloquial speech, but not in the polite speech that Shakespeare uses *(Shakespeare's Pronunciation,* New Haven, 1953, p. 88). E. J. Dobson
agrees that "the use of the raised sound was a vulgarism," but notes that it "might
occasionally make its way into the speech of higher classes..." *(English Pronunciation 1500-1700,* Oxford, 1957, II, 640). Dobson also indicates that "queen"
and "quean" appear as homophones on a number of contemporary lists.
   Whether or not this pun was actually intended on the Elizabethan stage, it
seems to be implied when Antony says, "I must from this enchanting queen
break off" (1.2.132), and it is also an innuendo in the exchange between Pompey
and Enobarbus in II,vi:

> *Pom.* And I have heard Apollodorus carried—
> *Eno.* No more of that! He did so.
> *Pom.*   What, I pray you?
> *Eno.* A certain queen to Caesar in a mattress.
>   (2.6.69-71)

We can perhaps see an instance here of covert puns setting off meanings already
present in our minds. Thomas Heywood very obviously plays on "queen" and
"quean" in the card-game of *A Woman Kilde with Kindnesse* (probably per-
formed in 1603—see Chambers, *Elizabethan Stage,* III, 342):

> *Wend.* I am a Knaue.
> *Nicke.* Ile sweare it.
> *Anne.* I a Queene.
> *Fr.* A quean thou shouldst say: wel the cards are mine,
>   They are the grosest paire that ere I felt.

(See *The Dramatic Works of Thomas Heywood,* London, J. Pearson, 1874, II,
123.)

The Pillar of the World: *Antony and Cleopatra* in Shakespeare's Development

by Julian Markels

The play is built upon the opposition of public and private values.[1] However we name them—love or honour, lust or empire—we know from the moment of Philo's opening speech that the issue before us is the form in which this opposition is to be resolved. It is usually said that Mark Antony is confronted by a choice between the values represented by Cleopatra and those represented by Octavius Caesar; and that however inadequate either value might be, he resolves this conflict by choosing Cleopatra and giving up the world. Instead I shall argue in this book that Mark Antony is disciplined in the distinctive vision of the play, wherein he is challenged either to choose between the opposed values represented by Cleopatra and Octavius or not to choose between them; and that instead of choosing, he resolves the conflict by striving equally toward both values and rhythmically making each one a measure and condition of the other. The result of his effort is that instead of becoming more "effeminate,"

[1]Some representative readings of the play may be found in A. C. Bradley, *Oxford Lectures on Poetry* (London, 1909), pp. 279-310; Maurice Charney, *Shakespeare's Roman Plays* (Cambridge, Mass., 1961), pp. 79-141; John F. Danby, *Poets on Fortune's Hill* (London, 1952), pp. 128-52; Willard Farnham, *Shakespeare's Tragic Frontier* (Berkeley, Calif., 1950), pp. 139-205; M. W. MacCallum, *Shakespeare's Roman Plays and Their Background* (London, 1910), pp. 300-453; Brents Stirling, *Unity in Shakespearean Tragedy* (New York, 1956), pp. 157-92; D. A. Traversi, *Shakespeare: The Roman Plays* (Stanford, Calif., 1963), pp. 79-203; and Mark Van Doren, *Shakespeare* (New York, 1953), pp. 230-42.

as in North's Plutarch, Shakespeare's Antony grows larger in manhood until he can encompass both Rome and Egypt, affirming the values that both have taught him until both are fulfilled. Then his death comes, as Cleopatra's does later, not as dissolution but as transcendence, a sign of his having approached as close to immortality as a poet may dare to imagine by becoming everything that it was in him to be. That I think is why the lovers' deaths produce a feeling of exaltation that so many critics find unique in Shakespeare. In the concrete detail of the play's rendition, these deaths are not permitted to break the continuity of existence. Antony kills himself with his own world-sharing sword, yet does not complete the work, so that he may be left to die upon a kiss, which in turn is not quite so much to die as to "melt" and "discandy."[2] Cleopatra desires death, like a "lover's pinch," to satisfy her immortal longing. She has found a means of death that will cause neither inward pain nor outward disfigurement; and she succeeds so well that in the embrace of the asp she merely "looks like sleep." For her and Antony death is not a limitation but a transformation of existence into a state of peace where the energy and the sweetness of life are at last unfettered. Their deaths signify not that one half of life is well lost for another but that both halves are found at last and hinged upon each other, in order that the whole world may be won.

This powerful element of transcendence in the death of the lovers, grounded as it is in their effort to reconcile public and private values by refusing to choose between them, marks an important stage in Shakespeare's development, and perhaps cannot begin to be understood outside the context of the Shakespearean canon. For one thing, the special poise in Shakespeare's treatment of death in this play suggests a familiar continuum. On the one hand, Antony and Cleopatra actually die, like the protagonists of the great tragedies, their physical deaths constituting a measure of providential judgment for their fully revealed human frailty. On the other hand, the tone of apotheosis in which their deaths are invested is in the symbolic key of Shakespeare's last plays, where death is no longer conceived naturalistically within the framework of a providential order, as in the tragedies, and is therefore no longer functional in the drama.

[2]On the general effect of this vein of imagery, see especially D. A. Traversi, *An Approach to Shakespeare* (London, 1938), pp. 116-27. But cf. Danby, *Poets on Fortune's Hill*, pp. 128-52.

Here as elsewhere *Antony and Cleopatra* goes far to bridge the difference between Shakespearean tragedy and romance.

Shakespeare's treatment of death in this play, moreover, is not simply a virtuoso performance isolated from the remainder of his concerns. There is a connection between the way the lovers die and the way they have lived, and their rewarding effort to reconcile public and private values locates *Antony and Cleopatra* on the central line of Shakespeare's development, where he is markedly concerned with this conflict of values in his history plays and Roman plays, in *Hamlet* and *King Lear* especially among the tragedies, and finally in *The Winter's Tale* and *The Tempest*. About this aspect of the play as well, it will be useful here to make a preliminary sketch of the argument to be developed in the following pages. Shakespeare's mind was formed in a community that felt itself to be achieving a precarious cultural and political unity after a devastating period of internal strife, and it was natural that early in his career Shakespeare, like many of his countrymen, should focus his attention on the two related problems of order in the state, and of the king's vocation in upholding that order. He began with a firm commitment to the doctrine that temporal order and the king's role are integrally related because both are divinely sanctioned and oriented.[3] But as he applied this doctrine to the presumed facts of history given him by his culture and to the facts of human nature discovered by his art, he came to question the divine self-regulating efficacy of a world order that had shown itself capable of such extensive breakdown as to provide him with the subject matter of his history plays. Simply the writing of such chronicle plays as Shakespeare's *Henry VI* and *Henry IV* cycles, instead of traditional morality plays or epics, served in fact to secularize the idea of world order, and to acknowledge politics as a fallen human activity rather than a divine sacrament. It is true that the chronicle plays typically attempt to picture the vicissitudes of politics

---

[3]Everybody who touches on this subject is indebted first of all to E. M. W. Tillyard, *The Elizabethan World Picture* (London, 1943) and *Shakespeare's History Plays* (London, 1951), as well as to Theodore Spencer, *Shakespeare and the Nature of Man* (Cambridge, Mass., 1942). The present book argues, if not directly with Tillyard and Spencer, then with the excessive influence of their work upon subsequent Shakespearean criticism. It argues also with an interpretation of the Roman plays that anticipates the work of Tillyard and Spencer: James E. Philips, Jr., *The State in Shakespeare's Greek and Roman Plays* (New York, 1940).

as the temporal reflection of a providential scheme. But their subject is disorder in the human community, and first of all they are called upon to dramatize the human causes and consequences of disorder. The more coherent and effective they were to become as plays, the more vividly they had to reveal the personal character of the king, both in weakness and in strength, as the best available warrant for order in the kingdom. As this process of aesthetic growth took place, as the chronicle plays sharpened and refined their concern for the relationship between personal character and public order, they began implicitly to conceive the state not allegorically, as a work of God, but dramatically, as a work of art. The England of Shakespeare's history plays depends for her health and destiny upon the specifically human talents, the shaping imagination of her Richards and her Henrys. These men may claim divine stewardship for themselves, and others may claim it for them: but the program of the plays is to show how they use their human power, for better or for worse, to mold their country's character by making her history.

When the state becomes a work of art, so does the person; and one of the striking elements in Shakespeare's history plays is the self-consciousness with which he invests his heroes. A passage from Burckhardt's *The Civilization of the Renaissance in Italy* will suggest the background for this phenomenon:

> In the Middle Ages both sides of human consciousness—that which was turned within and that which was turned without—lay as though dreaming or half awake beneath a common veil....Man was conscious of himself only as a member of a race, people, party, family, or corporation—only through some general category. It is in Italy that this veil dissolved first; there arose an *objective* treatment and consideration of the State and of all the things of this world, and at the same time the *subjective* side asserted itself with corresponding emphasis. Man became a spiritual *individual,* and recognized himself as such.[4]

Burckhardt is speaking of developments in Italy during the fourteenth and fifteenth centuries, and his remarks are relevant to Shakespeare's treatment of British history during the same period. It is a commonplace that in Shakespeare's history plays from *Richard II* to *Henry V* we see many facets of the transition

---

[4]Jacob Burckhardt, *The Civilization of the Renaissance in Italy* (New York, 1914), p. 129.

from a medieval to a modern conception of national politics and public life, especially in the career of Prince Hal. Henry Boling-broke and his son Hal, in contrast to Richard II and Hotspur, respectively, begin to conceive the state as an object of deliberate policy instead of ritual passion. Their desire to undertake foreign campaigns in order to distract their subjects from domestic rival-ries, and thereby to unite the nation behind them, typifies their sophisticated statecraft. With what the Elizabethans would have called a similarly Machiavellian adroitness, in their personal conduct they play shrewdly imagined roles in relation to their subjects, Prince Hal to such an extent that it is impossible to sep-arate the man from the self-dramatized public image. In his open-ing soliloquy, in his several claims for the educational value of his tavern life, in his trying the crown for size and his prompt defense of this premature experiment, and in his strained attempt at democratic comradeship with the common soldiers in *Henry V,* Hal is continuously stage-managing his effects and theatrically improvising his character as he goes along. Whatever might be his exact porportion of histrionic calculation at any given moment, he is almost never free of that pagan impulse to shape himself in images that he announced in his opening soliloquy....

Here I suggest only that for Shakespeare as he matures, the political leader's impulse toward self-dramatization becomes problematical, along with political order itself, as inseparable parts of a single awareness. The earlier concern for the perma-nence of order is progressively subordinated to a concern for that discrepancy between public and private values that *Antony and Cleopatra* is to call by the names of Rome and Egypt. In the history plays it is clear that the king's vocation, in order to deserve its divine sanction, requires the subordination of private values to that "ceremony" of the public world that King Henry V ex-plains in a notable speech of regret after he has purged himself, as Prince Hal, both of his earlier image of himself and of Falstaff. In fact, the friction between character and "ceremony" underlies the protagonist's self-dramatization as he tries to satisfy the public demands made upon him. This personal conflict between private and public loyalties influences in turn the ongoing politics of order, to complete a vicious circle: Shakespeare comes to recognize that the protagonist's histrionics may themselves constitute an original public fact, a cause rather than a symptom of political instability. This perception, fundamental to *Richard II,* is explored and enlarged in *Julius Caesar, Hamlet,* and *King Lear,* ... In these plays political ethics, and especially the psychological basis for ethics, become as important as the structure of public order. The private lives of Richard, Brutus, Hamlet, and Lear are threatened by self-dramatization no less regularly, and no less independently, than their political communities are subject to the vicissitudes of rebellion, usurpation, and anarchy. Character and society keep failing each other more and more, until the circle is broken in *King Lear.* There the self-dramatization of an aging king begins the dissolution of public order; once under way, the public disorder intensifies the private; and the fearful point is reached where each must complete itself separately, at the edge of doom, before public and private life both can be reconstituted. In *King Lear* public and private values, and beyond those values good and evil themselves, no longer are conceived in causal relations with each other; all virtues and flaws have become original and autonomous. If we can speak at all of divine providence in *King Lear,* we cannot say that it guarantees the continuity of political order, but only that it underwrites the existence of Cordelia as well as Edmund, so that life may continue if man chooses. Order and disorder, both public and private, are shown to be ineradicable potentialities of life; and personal self-dramatization is separated from politics and made an independent problem of vocation.

So much of Shakespeare's career falls into place in *King Lear,* and *King Lear* is so great a play in its own right, that it is difficult not to conclude that Shakespeare's development ends and culminates there. But this view impoverishes Shakespeare, whose development does not culminate anywhere but goes on through *Antony and Cleopatra* and other plays, to end where he ends, with *The Tempest.* In that development *Antony and Cleopatra* goes beyond *King Lear*—not above it but beyond it, to break new ground, and to fill out the whole contour of Shakespeare's development. The opposite of self-dramatization, Regan herself tells us in *King Lear,* is self-knowledge. By the time Lear achieves what measure of self-knowledge he is granted, he wants the safety of a "wall'd prison" to protect his personal accomplishment from any further threat of public life. One reason he is denied even this rescue is that Shakespeare has come to see that self-knowledge is not a condition but a process, like life itself, in which public and private values must remain in continuing negotiation with each other and in which not even the old and wise are permitted a separate peace, as Prospero will come to recognize. Meanwhile Shakespeare creates in Antony a character whose earned self-knowledge does not result in a desire to renounce the world for the safety of Lear's prison, but instead a desire to remain in the world, and, since it must continue to suffer his flaws, a magnanimous insistence upon giving freely to his world of his strength, virtue, and treasure as well. By accepting fully his own imperfection along with the world's, Antony is able to remain unprotected, and to let what goodness he has earned perform whatever acts of magnanimity are possible. For Shakespeare in *Antony and Cleopatra,* then, self-knowledge and the virtue it entails become not a place but a pathway, continually renewed in and through public action; and Shakespeare's progression from *King Lear* to *Antony and Cleopatra* is toward this conception, with its corollary vision of the immortal joining of public and private values.

Antony and Cleopatra: The Heroic Context

by Reuben A. Brower

The focus in the death scenes of both Antony and Cleopatra is on the "noble act" as it was variously interpreted by writers in the heroic tradition from Homer to the humanist translators and imitators. No listing of authors or works by which Shakespeare may have been "influenced" can account for the complexity with which the brave and noble action is enriched in *Antony and Cleopatra*. The source of the enrichment lies beyond the reach of research, in the power by which Shakespeare poetically reinterpreted North's version of Plutarch.

Shakespeare had almost certainly read Daniel's *The Tragedy of Cleopatra,* and perhaps also the Countess of Pembroke's translation of Garnier, *The Tragedy of Antonie;*[1] but he could not have found in these long-winded and relatively simple plays anything like a model for *Antony and Cleopatra.* The titles indicate a major difference from Shakespeare—neither author was capable of embracing the two dramas in a single vision. Both works are related to the moral narrative tradition of the *Mirror for Magistrates,* though the "complaints" are given a superficially Senecan look by assigning speakers and interspersing the lamentations and moralizing reflections with messenger speeches and with choruses on mythological parallels, on the "healthful succour" of Death, on the evils of declining greatness and disorder. Of the two plays, *Antonie* is of the more purely complaining type, with many direct and flat lamentations by the hero on his ruin through passion

[1]All quotations of the two plays are from the texts (of 1595 and of 1599, respectively) in Bullough, v.

and ruthless destiny. Terms common in Elizabethan heroic tragedy appear frequently: greatness, glory, passions, prowess, honour, reason. (A similar list could be compiled from Daniel's play.) There are fragmentary glimpses of Shakespeare's major theme, for example, when Antonie grieves over the loss of his "great Empire,"

> scarse maister of thy selfe,
> Late maister of so many Nations...   129

or when he confesses with earnest ineptness "So I me lost" (1158).

Daniel, less earnest than the Countess of Pembroke, writes with more grace and occasionally with dramatic power. In one of the better passages, his Cleopatra touches on the Shakespearian motif of the mystery of self-betrayal:[2]

> Am I the woman whose inventive pride,
> Adorn'd like *Isis*, scorned mortalitie?
> Is't I would have my frailetie so belide,
> That flattery could perswade I was not I?
>   32-6

The admirable closing lines by the chorus in Daniel's play may have set Shakespeare thinking about another mystery:

> Is greatnesse of this sort,
> That greatnesse greatnesse marres,
> And wrackes it selfe, selfe driven
> On Rockes of her owne might?
> Doth Order order so
> Disorders overthrow?   1748-1753

But what a difference, compared with

> Now all labour
> Mars what it does; yea, very force entangles
> Itself with strength.   IV.xiv.47-49

In Daniel, contradictory impulses are thoughtfully—and not ineffectively—presented in the most general terms; in Shake-

---

[2]"In the *Cleopatra* of 1594 [date of first publication] the heroine offers much self-analysis in long passages of soliloquy that follow the right Senecan pattern." Farnham, *Shakespeare's Tragic Frontier,* p. 158. For further discussion of parallels with Daniel see Bullough, v. 235-38. See also, for soliloquies in Seneca, Chapter III, pp. 160-63, 167.

speare, they are expressed from within, through muscular thwartings of image and through hesitations of speech mirroring a mind in the act of choosing: "Seal then, and all is done." Although a number of parallels between Shakespeare and Daniel have been pointed out, they hardly add up to a conception or an attitude that Shakespeare "took over" from *The Tragedy of Cleopatra.* A more likely explanation is that certain sorts of heroic diction would be used in any Elizabethan version of the "fall" of Antony and Cleopatra.

From the discussion of Plutarch in an earlier chapter, it can be assumed that Shakespeare's reading of North had something to do with his focusing his double tragedy on the theme of nobility. "Noble," the word that re-echoes throughout Shakespeare's play and the *Life of Marcus Antonius,* occurs rarely in the plays of Daniel and the Countess of Pembroke, though there is one interesting example in *Antonie.* Shortly after saying that he is "like Hercules," Antonie concludes, bathetically,

> Die, die I must: I must a noble death,
> A glorious death unto my succour call...
> 1238-1239

We may think that it would be hard to read North without saying, "Noble Antony," though we might not do so, if we were not already familiar with Shakespeare's play; for the total impression of Antony's character in Plutarch is much less admirable. All the elements of soldierly (not moral) nobility in Shakespeare's portrait turn up in North-Plutarch: the "noble exploits," the eagerness to "attempt great enterprises," the "desire to win honour." A single comment sums up Antony's martial qualities with Elizabethan fullness of expression.[3]

> Antonius did many noble actes of a valliant and wise Captaine: but specially in one battell, where he compassed in the enemies behind, giving them the victorie that fought against them, whereby he afterwards had such honorable reward, as his valliantnes deserved.
> VI. 4

With similar over-emphasis North writes that Julius Caesar at Pharsalia "gave Antonius the leading of the left wing as the valiantest man and skilfullest souldier of all those he had about

[3]North adds "noble." "Valiant and wise" is for *tolmés;* "valliantnes" is for Amyot's *vertu,* Plutarch's *aristeia.*

him." The higher qualities that Plutarch valued in other heroes, courtesy, liberality, and greatness of mind, belong also to Shakespeare's Antony. But the more vulgar traits of North's "plain soldier," the cruelty, the weakness for "enticing men's wives," and the outright lustfulness are minimized in *Antony and Cleopatra*.[4]

For the contrast between Shakespearian complexity and the simplicity of North and Plutarch, consider this typical observation on Cleopatra's love:

> Then beganne this pestilent plague and mischiefe of Cleopatraes love...againe to kindle, and to be in force, so soone as Antonius came neere unto Syria.

The next sentence is one that may have suggested to Shakespeare his major moral theme, the defeat of reason by passion:

> And in the ende, the horse of the minde as Plato termeth it, that is so hard of rayne (I meane the unreyned lust of concupiscence) did put out of Antonius heade, all honest and commendable thoughts...
>
> VI. 36

In another passage, Octavius says that "Antonius was not master of himself, but that Cleopatra had brought him beside himself by her charms and amorous poisons...." But in North as in Plutarch, these and similar judgements remain mere judgements. Shakespeare alone gave dramatic life to the history of a noble mind defeated, not by "charms and poisons," but by itself. In the comparison of Antony and Demetrius North very nearly defines Shakespeare's subject, but misses its tragic meaning: "Antony by his incontinence, did no hurt but to himself."

The treatment of Antony's death in the play shows more exactly how well Shakespeare adjusted his borrowings to fit his special vision. "And for their deaths," Plutarch concludes at the end of the comparison,

> a man can not praise the one nor the other, but yet Demetrius death the more reproachefull. For he suffered him selfe to be taken prisoner, and when he was sent away to be kept in a straunge place, he had the hart to live yet three yeare longer, to serve his mouth and bellie, as brute beastes doe. Antonius on the other side slue him selfe, (to confesse a troth) cowardly, and miserably, to his great paine and griefe: and yet was it before his bodie came into his enemies hands.
>
> VI. 93

[4]MacCallum observes that Shakespeare "has idealized his model, but it is by reading the soul of greatness through the sordid details...," p. 337.

Plutarch grants, a bit reluctantly, that Antony's death was less "reproachefull" by a primitive heroic standard: better to die than be a captive. The difference in tragic depth can be illustrated from a single detail in the two versions of Antony's last speech. "And as for him selfe," Antony says to Cleopatra in North,

> that she should not lament nor sorowe for the miserable chaunge of his fortune at the end of his dayes: but rather that she should thinke him the more fortunate, for the former triumphes and honors he had received, considering that while he lived he was the noblest and greatest Prince of the world, and that now he was overcome, not cowardly, but valiantly, a Romane by an other Romane.
>
>   VI. 80

By dropping "an other" from Plutarch's last phrase, Shakespeare gives an altogether new meaning to Antony's consoling words: "a Roman by a Roman/ Valiantly vanquish'd." Through this slight omission, Antony is made to triumph in his singular way, and the peculiar "nobility" of his death is given precise expression.

Where Shakespeare rises above Plutarch particularly is in his survey of the total tragic situation, the view summed up in Caesar's final comment. "Pity" for the destructiveness of heroic enterprise and wondering appreciation of "glory" are both necessary for wise evaluation of "high events as these," for the kind of understanding central to heroic poetry in the Graeco-Roman tradition. This is the tragic vision that Shakespeare has dramatized in *Antony and Cleopatra,* and to which he alludes in all his greater tragedies. The attitude expressed toward the hero's *agon* would be familiar to a reader of the *Iliad,* of which Shakespeare had some knowledge, or to a reader of Greek tragedy, which Shakespeare knew only through the distorted versions of Seneca and his translators. But if Shakespeare had not read Sophocles, he had read Virgil, the greatest poet of "pity" and "glory" in the ancient world.

It is hard to believe that Shakespeare's play would have taken the form it did without the felt presence of the *Aeneid* in so much Elizabethan narrative and dramatic poetry. Whether there is or is not a direct connection,[5] Virgil's tragedy of two heroic lovers, both heads of state and both intensely noble, offers a relevant comparison for exploring and characterizing the quality of Shakespeare's play. *Antony and Cleopatra* is an imaginative sequel to

---

[5]There is a brief reference to the Dido and Aeneas parallel in Knight, *The Imperial Theme,* p. 286. See also Schanzer, *Problem Plays,* pp. 158-59.

the *Aeneid:* what might have happened had Aeneas stayed in Carthage and not fulfilled his fate. Like Aeneas, Antony cannot altogether put behind him the "Roman thought" of the role that historical destiny (*fata Romana*) and the heroic code require him to play. But it is the role given to Cleopatra by Shakespeare that becomes clearer through comparison with the *Aeneid.*

Where others had written tragedies of Antony *or* Cleopatra, Shakespeare writes his double tragedy, adapting to Cleopatra Dido's role of temptress and heroic queen, and like Virgil, daringly combining an intimate drama of love with a historical drama of epic scale. The parallel in subject is the more striking, since *Antony and Cleopatra* moves toward the establishment of Augustus and the *pax Augusta,* both of which Virgil's poem celebrates. But in his characterization of Octavius and the makers of the new order, Shakespeare casts a cold eye on the course of empire. (There is a deeper irony in Virgil's sense of the cost of the whole Roman achievement.)

Cleopatra is not only like Dido a woman capable of jealous fury; she also equals her lover in nobility, as Dido equalled Aeneas. Both women are conscious of their responsibilities as "president" of a kingdom. Both belong to the company of "the greatest," and both have a high regard for reputation, for *fama.* But there is no way of tracing how Shakespeare was led to create a Cleopatra so different from the woman North describes as a "pestilent plague and a mischief." Though the *Life* includes two references to Cleopatra's "noble mind," there is nothing in Plutarch to match the sustained nobility of Shakespeare's Cleopatra in the later scenes of the play. It is barely possible that Shakespeare found a hint of the parallel to Dido in *The Tragedie of Antonie:*

> And now of me an Image great shall goe
> Under the earth to bury there my woe.
>   1959-1960

> et nunc magna mei sub terras ibit imago.
>   *Aeneid,* IV. 654

Perhaps in writing Iras' lines,

> Finish, good lady. The bright day is done,
> And we are for the dark...

he had, as we noted in another chapter, a dim memory of Surrey's translation,

> But let us die for thus: and in this sort
> It liketh us to seek the shadowes darck.
>
> IV. 880-881

Or perhaps the parallel occurred to Shakespeare simply because he had read both Virgil[6] and Plutarch.

Marlowe's *Dido Queene of Carthage,* we have already suggested,[7] offered the most likely example for the Shakespearian blend in *Antony and Cleopatra* of the Virgilian heroic and the Ovidian erotic:

> Stout love, in mine arms make thy Italy,
> Whose crown and kingdom rests at thy command...
>
> I'll frame me wings of wax, like Icarus,
> And o'er his ships will soar unto the sun
> That they may melt, and I fall in his arms;
> Or else I'll make a prayer unto the waves
> That I may swim to him, like Triton's niece,
> O Anna, fetch Arion's harp,
> That I may tice a dolphin to the shore
> And ride upon his back unto my love!
>
> III. iv. 56-57; V. i. 243-250

In Cleopatra Shakespeare created a heroine who was Ovidian in being amusing as well as heroic and amorous, and in giving herself up to contradictory passions and changing moods. Her wit sometimes has an Ovidian turn of phrase and Ovid's epigrammatic sharpness:

> There would he anchor his aspect, and die
> With looking on his life...

Celerity is never more admired than by the negligent...(The second instance is the kind of thrust Ovid's Helen is fond of.) Cleopatra might also be described as a blend of Ovid's sophisticated woman of Rome with the "immortal" Helen of Marlowe's *Faustus.* Her metamorphosis in the last scene of Shakespeare's play is only Ovid transposed in a higher key. The heroine of this historical myth, like Ovid's Achilles, does not become a flower, a tree, or a bird, but "immortal," all "fire and air," a star-like di-

---

[6]See Chapter II, pp. 99-103. The Arden editor notes a possible parallel with Stanyhurst's *Aeneis* in the "reneges" of I. i. 8.

[7] Chapter II, p. 113.

vinity, mother goddess and serpentine genius of sleep. This is the super-woman who dreamed Antony's apotheosis, which is Ovidian too in its grostesque beauty: "His face was as the heav'ns, and therein stuck/ A sun and moon"—a colossus who "bestrid the Ocean," half Neptune and half Jove. Both transformations are symbolic of the inexpressible greatness that Cleopatra attained by heroic death, and that Antony had lost, to regain in a new form. But though Cleopatra has her tragic dissatisfaction, her "desolation," and though Shakespeare invests her career, like Antony's, with the tragic sense of the destructiveness inherent in greatness, she never undergoes, as Antony does, Dido's passionate inner experience of lost "reputation." It is Antony alone who is a truly tragic figure in the tradition of ancient and Renaissance heroic tragedy. Like Homer's Achilles, he is driven by *Até*, and like Chapman's Achilles, he suffers the loss of inner "sovereignty." But he is joined with Cleopatra in "glory." The "wonderful," the quality that Renaissance critics admired in heroic poetry, is salient in our total impression of *Antony and Cleopatra*, most variously heroic of all Shakespearian tragedies. The ease with which Shakespeare moves in this play from heroic tragedy to divine comedy, both high and low, shows that he had recovered for modern literature the freedom of Homer.

Antony and Cleopatra:
A Shakespearian Adjustment

by John F. Danby

At each stage in his development Shakespeare displays a surprising capacity for renewal. Let us assume that *Antony and Cleopatra* comes after *King Lear*, that it goes with *Coriolanus*, and that both it and *Coriolanus* immediately precede the so-called "last period." Between *Antony and Cleopatra* and the plays that have gone before there is no obvious connection in theme or technique. At the same time, only Plutarch links it with *Coriolanus*. Nothing in it would normally prepare us for *Cymbeline* or *The Winter's Tale* to follow. This apparent isolation is one of the main obstacles to a correct focus on the play. There seems to be a break in the internal continuity of the Shakespearian series—a continuity of series which stretches, I think, from *Henry VI* to *King Lear* at least, and which could possibly be extended to include *Timon:* though here again there is something of a lesion, and special factors, external to the "inner biography" of Shakespeare as a playwright, might have to be invoked to explain all that is happening. *Timon,* however, it might be granted, is the aftermath of *King Lear*. Can the same be said about *Antony and Cleopatra?*

I

To describe the swiftness of *Antony and Cleopatra* we need to draw on the imagery of the cinema. There is more cinematic movement, more panning, tracking, and playing with the camera, more mixing of shots than in any other of Shakespeare's tragedies.

"*Antony and Cleopatra:* A Shakespearian Adjustment." From *Elizabethan and Jacobean Poets*, by John F. Danby (London: Faber and Faber Ltd., 1952), pp. 128-51. Reprinted by permission of Faber and Faber Ltd.

At the same time the technique is always under deliberate, almost cool, control. *Antony and Cleopatra* has none of the haphazardies of *Pericles* nor any of the plot-imposed vagaries of the last period. The technique is inwardly related to the meaning Shakespeare has to express. What is indicated is not enervation or indifference, but rather what Coleridge recognized as "giant power," an "angelic strength."

The swift traverse of time and space has often been commented upon. There is also the mixing. Egypt is called up vividly in Rome by Enobarbus's descriptions. Rome is always felt as a real presence in Egypt. On the frontiers of Empire Ventidius discusses what repercussions his victories will have on the people at staff-head-quarters. Equally the present is interpenetrated by the past. Antony's past, particularly, is always powerfully put before us:

> Antony,
> Leave thy lascivious wassails. When thou once
> Wast beaten from Modena, where thou slew'st
> Hirtius and Pansa, consuls, at thy heels
> Did famine follow, whom thou fought'st against
> Though daintily brought up, with patience more
> Than savages could suffer; thou didst drink
> The stale of horses, and the gilded puddle
> Which beasts would cough at; thy palate then did deign
> The roughest berry on the rudest hedge;
> Yea, like the stag, when snow the pasture sheets,
> It is reported thou didst eat strange flesh,
> Which some did die to look on.   (I.iv.55-68)

So, too, is Cleopatra's:

> I found you as a morsel cold upon
> Dead Caesar's trenchar; nay, you were a fragment
> Of Cneius Pompey's; besides what hotter hours,
> Unregister'd in vulgar fame, you have
> Luxuriously pick'd out.   (III.ix.116-120)

The hinterland of the quarrels that alternately divide and bring together again the triumvirate is constantly being suggested, troubles, truces, and manoeuvres that go back (like Cleopatra's love-affairs) to Julius Caesar's days. In no other of his plays is Shakespeare at such pains to suggest the stream of time past and its steady course through the present. In the public world of Roman affairs this is especially so. In the other world of Cleopatra the same suggestion of perspective always frames what is said and done. Is Antony merely the last of a long succession of such lovers? Or is this affair singular and unique as all love-affairs claim to be? Not enough weight has been given in recent assessments of the play to the ambiguity which invests everything in Egypt equally with all things in Rome. Yet this ambiguity is central to Shakespeare's experience in the play. If it is wrong to see the "mutual pair" as a strumpet and her fool, it is also wrong to see them as a Phoenix and a Turtle.

In addition to the swiftness and the variety of the impacts, and the interpenetration of the parts of time and space as they mix in the speech of the people immediately before us, there is also the added burden which Shakespeare's "giant power" of compelling presentation imposes. The effects are at once those of a rapid impressionism and a careful lapidary enrichment. Each figure, however minor, has its moment when it comes up into the brilliant foreground light—the Soothsayer with his "infinite book of secrecy," the Old Man wishing "much joy o' the worm," Enobarbus describing the barge on the Nile, Lepidus asking "What manner o' thing is your crocodile?" Ventidius giving once for all the field-officer's view of the higher-ups, the Eunuch and the game of billiards, Dolabella, Octavia, even Fulvia whom we never see: the canvas seems covered with Constable's snow.

Another feature of Shakespeare's technique which makes for the impression of uniqueness might be pointed to here. Shakespeare seems to be innovating also in methods of character-portrayal. Some of the stage conventions, as described by Miss Bradbrook, do not seem to apply. Which, for example, are we to believe—what Caesar says about Antony after he is dead, or what he says about him, and his conduct towards him, while he is alive? What was Fulvia's "character," about whom we have such conflicting reports? Throughout the play we are forced by Shakespeare himself not to take comment at its face value. Judgments are more personal here than elsewhere. Goneril and Regan discussing their father's condition are reliable judges. Caesar, Antony, Enobarbus, the soldiers Demetrius and Philo, are not—or not to the same extent. Judgment knits itself back into character as it might do in Ibsen, and character issues from a mutable and ambiguous flux of things. Antony's momentary *agnorisis* can be generalized to cover the whole play:

> Sometimes we see a cloud that's dragonish;
> A vapour sometimes like a bear or lion,

A tower'd citadel, a pendant rock,
A forked mountain, or blue promontory,
With trees upon't, that nod unto the world
And mock our eyes with air: thou hast seen these signs;
They are black vespers pageants...
That which is now a horse, even with a thought
The rack dislimns, and makes it indistinct
As water is in water...
My good knave, Eros, now thy captain is
Even such a body: here I am Antony,
Yet cannot hold this visible shape, my knave.
(IV.xii.2-14)

There is something deliquescent in the reality behind the play. It is a deliquescence to the full display of which each judgment, each aspect pointed to, and each character, is necessary, always provided that no single one of these is taken as final. The proportion of comment and judgment on the central characters is higher in *Antony and Cleopatra* than anywhere else in Shakespeare. This further underlines its uniqueness and the difficulties of coming by an adequate final assessment. Antony and Cleopatra are presented in three ways. There is what is said about them; there is what they say themselves; there is what they do. Each of these might correspond to a different "level" of response. Each is in tension against the others. Each makes its continuous and insistent claim on the spectator for judgment in his own right. The pigments vividly opposed to each other on the canvas have to mix in the spectator's eye.

Underlying, however, the bewildering oscillations of scene, the overlapping and pleating of different times and places, the co-presence of opposed judgments, the innumerable opportunities for radical choice to intervene, there is, I think, a deliberate logic. It is this which gives the play its compact unity of effect and makes its movement a sign of angelic strength rather than a symptom of febrility. It is the logic of a peculiarly Shakespearian dialectic. Opposites are juxtaposed, mingled, married; then from the very union which seems to promise strength dissolution flows. It is the process of this dialectic—the central process of the play—which we must trace if we wish to arrive anywhere near Shakespeare's meaning.

II

The first scene opens with Philo's comment on the "dotage" of his general:

> those his goodly eyes
> That o'er the files and musters of the war
> Have glow'd like plated Mars: now bend, now turn
> The office and devotion of their view
> Upon a tawny front; his captain's heart,
> Which in the scuffles of great fights hath burst
> The buckles on his breast, reneges all temper,
> And is become the bellows and the fan
> To cool a gipsy's lust.   (I.i.2-10)

Nothing more has time to be said. Antony and Cleopatra themselves appear. Their first words express the essence of romantic love, a tacit contradiction of all that Philo seems to have just suggested:

> *Cleo.* If it be love indeed, tell me how much.
> *Ant.* There's beggary in the love that can be reckon'd.
> *Cleo.* I'll set a bourn how far to be belov'd.
> *Ant.* Then must thou needs find out new heaven, new earth.
>   (I.i.14-17)

Again immediately, an attendant announces the arrival of news from Rome. The atmosphere of the Egyptian court changes. We see the opposite effects of the intrusion on the two it most concerns. Antony will not hear the messengers. Cleopatra insists that he shall. Antony is taunted with a wicked caricature of what the news might be, and of the relation in which he stands to Rome. Yet the version is sufficiently like to make Antony blush—from anger, or shame, or both:

> Your dismission
> Is come from Caesar; therefore hear it, Antony,
> Where's Fulvia's process? Caesar's would I say? both?
> Call in the messengers. As I am Egypt's queen,
> Thou blushest, Antony, and that blood of thine
> Is Caesar's homager; else so thy cheek pays shame
> When shrill-tongued Fulvia scolds.   (I.i.26-32)

Antony's reaction is to pitch his romantic vows higher still, as-
serting his independence of Rome in terms that should leave no
doubt as to where he stands:

> Let Rome in Tiber melt, and the wide arch
> Of the rang'd empire fall! Here is my space.
> Kingdoms are clay; our dungy earth alike
> Feeds beast as man; the nobleness of life
> Is to do thus; when such a mutual pair
> And such a twain can do't, in which I bind
> On pain of punishment, the world to weet
> We stand up peerless.   (I.i.33-40)

This again has all the ring of absolute and heroic self-committal.
Cleopatra's reply, however, is typical both of herself and of the
ambivalence that runs through everything in the play:

> Excellent falsehood!
> Why did he marry Fulvia and not love her?
> I'll seem the fool I am not; Antony
> Will be himself.   (I.i.40-43)

Her first words might be oxymoron or plain disbelief. The next
call up the vista of Antony's past, with its broken pledges and un-
conscious insincerities—if they were no more. Her last words are
highly ambiguous and turn the whole situation upside-down:
she is the helpless creature wilfully blinding and deceiving herself, Antony is the self-contained and calculating manipulator
of her weaknesses. In replying, Antony is like the man innocent
of ju-jutsu who thinks he is pushing when really he is being
pulled:

> But stirr'd by Cleopatra.
> Now, for the love of Love and her soft hours,
> Let's not confound the time with conference harsh…
> …What sport tonight?   (I.i.43-47)

Shakespeare gives the operative lines a subtle falsity of note
that could equally indicate hearty play-acting, slightly awkward
self-consciousness, or wilful evasion. Cleopatra's answer is realist
and comes with a new urgency:

> Hear the ambassadors.   (I.i.48)

It drives Antony also to something we can recognize as more fully
himself—something that is perceptive and tinged with the master-
ful as well as the reckless:

> Fie, wrangling queen!
> Whom everything becomes, to chide, to laugh,
> To weep; whose every passion fully strives
> To make itself in thee fair and admir'd.
> No messenger, but thine; and all alone,
> Tonight we'll wander through the streets and note
> The qualities of people. Come, my queen;
> Last night you did desire it: speak not to us.
>
> (I.i.48-55)

This is not only Antony's view of Cleopatra's character, and a reliable account of what she is really like. It is also an expression of the deliquescent reality at the heart of the play which incarnates itself most completely in the persons of the hero and heroine. After Antony's speech, with this two-fold authority it bears, the comment of the soldiers seems peculiarly limited and out of place:

> *Dem.* Is Caesar with Antonius priz'd so slight?
> *Phil.* Sir, sometimes when he is not Antony,
> He comes too short of that great property
> Which still should go with Antony.
> *Dem.* I am full sorry
> That he approves the common liar, who
> Thus speaks of him at Rome; but I will hope
> Of better deeds tomorrow.   (I.i.56-62)

It serves to remind us, however, of the world that stands around the lovers, the world of the faithful soldier who can only understand the soldierly, the world of "the common liar" that enjoys the unpleasant "truth," the world, too, of Rome and Caesar that is radically opposed to the world of Egypt and Cleopatra.

The first scene is only slightly more than sixty lines long. Yet it is sufficient to illustrate all the main features of the play we have pointed to, and extensive enough to set up the swinging ambivalence—the alternatives and ambiguities constantly proposed to choice—which will govern and control our whole reaction to the play. There is the speed and oscillation, the interpenetration of Rome and Egypt and of present and past. Above all there is the dialectic marriage of the contraries and their dissolution through union. The jealousy of Cleopatra towards Fulvia, the outrage of Caesar to Antony's *amour propre*—these negative repulsions can serve to hold the mutual pair together as firmly as positive attractions. Antony and Cleopatra are opposed to the world that surrounds and isolates them. In this isolation their

union seems absolute, infinite, and self-sufficient. Yet the war
of the contraries pervades the love, too. In coming together they
lapse, slide, and fall apart unceasingly.

The outstanding achievement of the first scene is the way in
which it begins with the soldiers' condemnation and returns us
at the end to the same thing—allowing for this side eighteen lines
out of the sixty-two. Yet at the end we are no longer satisfied as to
the adequacy of what Demetrius and Philo say. Not that what they
say has been disproved by what we have seen of Antony and Cleopatra. They are and they remain a strumpet and her fool. To have
any judgment at all is to choose, apparently, either the judgment
of the soldiers at the beginning of the scene or the lovers' own
self-assessment that immediately follows it. (Coleridge chose the
former; Dr. Sitwell and Mr. Wilson Knight take the latter.) To
entertain either judgment, however, is not enough. The deliquescent truth is neither in them nor between them, but contains
both. *Antony and Cleopatra* is Shakespeare's critique of judgment.

Scene i played out romantic love and lovers' quarrels on a lofty
stage. It also gave the sharp local comment of the soldiery. Scene
ii takes the theme of love below-stairs and changes key. It also
gives the universal comment of the Soothsayer, with its suggestion
that everything is already decided, the tragedy is in the nature of
things, now is already over, the future past, the present always:

> In nature's infinite book of secrecy
> A little can I read...
> I make not but foresee....
> You have seen and prov'd a fairer former fortune
> Than that which is to approach.   (I.ii.11-36)

In place of the "romance" of love, Charmian, Iras, and Alexas
give the "reality." The reality in this case is a strong succession of
rich, powerful, and adequate males:

> Let me be married to three kings in a forenoon, and widow them
> all; let me have a child at fifty to whom Herod of Jewry may do
> homage; find me to marry with Octavius Caesar, and companion
> me with my mistress.

It reads like a parody of Cleopatra's aspirations, just as the women's
bickering and teasing of Alexas mimics Cleopatra's handling of
Antony:

> Alexas—come, his fortune, his fortune. O! let him marry a woman
> that cannot go, sweet Isis, I beseech thee; and let her die too, and
> give him a worse; and let worse follow worse, till the worst of all
> follow him laughing to his grave, fifty-fold a cuckold!

This seems a nightmare version of Antony's fate—the reflection
in a distorting mirror of the thoughts and feelings that course
through Antony after Cleopatra's desertion in the disastrous
sea-fight.

The group is interrupted in its fortune-telling by the entry of
Cleopatra. She is looking for Antony. Her remarks prepare us for
the different mood about to establish itself:

> Saw you my lord? ...
> He was disposed to mirth; but on the sudden
> A Roman thought hath struck him.
>
> (I.ii.86-91)

Antony is heard approaching. Cleopatra immediately goes off.
Now that he is coming she will refuse to see him.

When Antony appears he is surrounded by the messengers
from Rome and immersed in Roman affairs. He veers savagely
to the point of view both of the soldiers in the first scene and "the
common liar" in Rome. Throughout the play this is what marks
him off from Cleopatra and makes him a more complex meeting-
ground for the opposites than even she is herself. He can understand and respond to the appeal of Rome as much as he can understand and respond to Egypt:

> Speak to me home, mince not the general tongue;
> Name Cleopatra as she's called in Rome;
> Rail thou in Fulvia's phrase; and taunt my faults
> With such full license as both truth and malice
> Have power to utter. O! then we bring forth weeds
> When our quick winds lie still; and our ills told us
> Is as our earing. Fare thee well awhile...
> These strong Egyptian fetters I must break,
> Or lose myself in dotage.   (I.ii.113-126)

The second messenger brings news of Fulvia's death. It is characteristic of the play that what is hated during life should find

favour once it is dead. Later in this scene that is reported to be
the case with Pompey in the popular reaction to him:

> our slippery people—
> Whose love is never link'd to the deserter
> Till his deserts are past—begin to throw
> Pompey the great and all his dignities
> Upon his son.   (I.ii.198-202)

This is what happens, too, in Antony's case when, once he is dead,
Octavius sings his praises. It also happens when Cleopatra is
thought to have committed suicide and Antony flings from
vituperation to acclamation almost without pausing. It happens
now with Fulvia. Antony says:

> There's a great spirit gone! Thus did I desire it:
> What our contempts do often hurl' from us
> We wish it ours again; the present pleasure,
> By revolution lowering, does become
> The opposite of itself: she's good being gone.
> The hand could pluck her back that shov'd her on.
> I must from this enchanting queen break off.
>   (I.ii.131-137)

Typically, when he joins the general, Enobarbus summons all
the counter-arguments. To leave Egypt would be to kill Cleopatra. "She is cunning," Antony says, "past man's thought."
"Alack, sir, no," Enobarbus rejoins,

> her passions are made of nothing but the finest part of pure love.
> We cannot call her winds and waters sighs and tears; they are
> greater storms and tempests than almanacs can report: this cannot
> be cunning in her; if it be, she makes a shower of rain as well as
> Jove.   (I.ii.156-162)

Even if we read Enobarbus's words as irony, the double-irony
that works by virtue of the constant ambivalence in the play still
turns them back to something approaching the truth: and Cleopatra's real distress and anxiety over Antony's departure have
already cut through the scene like a knife. The ding-dong
continues:

> *Antony.* Would I had never seen her!
> *Enobarbus.* O, sir! you had then left unseen a wonderful piece of
>   work.
> *Antony.* Fulvia is dead.

> *Enobarbus.* Sir?
> *Antony.* Fulvia is dead.
> *Enobarbus.* Fulvia?
> *Antony.* Dead.
> *Enobarbus.* Why, sir, give the gods a thankful sacrifice…this
> grief is crown'd with consolation; your old smock brings forth
> a new petticoat.   (I.ii.163-181)

Antony, however, has made up his mind to go back to Rome.

Antony does go back to Rome—but not in the mood and not with the motives of thorough-going reformation in which he remains at the end of Scene ii. In Scene iii the alchemy of the Shakespearian process is further at work. It works to make Antony do the thing resolved upon but for reasons the very opposite of those which led him to the resolve. The scene of his departure is chosen for Cleopatra's most sincere avowal. Having tormented Antony beyond all bearing she suddenly breaks off with:

> Courteous lord, one word.
> Sir, you and I must part, but that's not it;
> Sir, you and I have loved, but there's not it;
> That you know well: something it is I would
> O my oblivion is a very Antony
> And I am all forgotten.   (I.iii.86-91)

Antony's final words in the scene almost catch the very idiom of *The Phoenix and the Turtle:*

> Let us go. Come.
> Our separation so abides and flies,
> That thou, residing here, go'st yet with me,
> And I, hence fleeting, here remain with thee.
> Away!   (I.iii.101-105)

It is, so to speak, the honeymoon of the contraries—only possible while the lovers are apart.

III

The first three scenes show how pervasive is that quality in technique and vision which we have called the Shakespearian "dialectic." It comes out in single images, it can permeate whole speeches, it governs the build-up inside each scene, it explains the way one scene is related to another. The word "dialectic," of course, is unfortunately post-Hegelian. The thing we wish to point to, however, in using the word, is Shakespearian. In *Antony and Cleopatra* Shakespeare needs the opposites that merge, unite, and fall apart. They enable him to handle the reality he is writing about—the vast containing opposites of Rome and Egypt, the World and the Flesh.

Rome is the sphere of the political. Shakespeare uses the contraries (long before Blake) to give some sort of rational account of the irrationals there involved. The common people, for example, is "the common liar." Antony has already noted that its love is "never link'd to the deserver till his deserts are past." Caesar, too, has his own cold knowledge of the same fact:

> It hath been taught us from the primal state
> That he which is was wished until he were;
> And the ebb'd man, ne'er loved till ne'er worth love,
> Comes dear'd by being lack'd. This common body,
> Like to the vagabond flag upon the stream,
> Goes to and back, lackeying the varying tide,
> To rot itself with motion.   (I.iv.41-47)

The great men, however, behave exactly as they say the commons do, too. With Antony, Fulvia becomes dear'd by being lack'd. In Caesar's case it is the same. The threat of Pompey makes him suddenly appreciate the grandeur of Antony's leadership, courage, and endurance. The magnanimous praise of Antony in Act V is only possible because Antony by then is dead. The law is general: judgment is a kind of accommodation to the irrational on reason's part:

> men's judgments are
> A parcel of their fortunes, and things outward
> Do draw the inward quality after them,
> To suffer all alike.   (III.ix.31-34)

Even soldierly "honour" is rooted in the ambiguous. When Pompey's man mentions his treacherous scheme for disposing of all Pompey's rivals at one blow (the rivals are also Pompey's guests on board ship), Pompey exclaims:

> Ah, this thou should'st have done
> And not have spoken on't. In me 'tis villainy;
> In thee't had been good service. Thou must know

> 'Tis not my profit that does lead mine honour;
> Mine honour it. Repent that e'er thy tongue
> Hath so betray'd thine act; being done unknown,
> I should have found it afterwards well done,
> But must condemn it now.   (II.vii.80-87)

The law is general because it reflects the nature of the terrene world—the tidal swing of the opposites on which all things balance in a motion that rots them away.

The self-destruction of things that rot with the motion which their own nature and situation dictate is almost obsessive with Shakespeare throughout the play. The political world is the manipulation of the common body they despise by the great men whom the commons can never love until they are safely rid of them. The pattern which remains constant in all the possible groupings is that of open conflict alternating with diseased truce, neither of them satisfactory:

> Equality of two domestic powers
> Breeds scrupulous faction. The hated, grown to strength,
> Are newly grown to love....
> And quietness, grown sick of rest, would purge
> By any desperate change.   (I.iii.47-54)

Compacts between the great men merely represent the temporary sinking of lesser enmities in front of greater:

>   lesser enmities give way to greater.
> Were't not that we stand up against them all
> 'Twere pregnant they should square amongst themselves.
>   (II.i.43-45)

Pompey's is a correct appreciation. It is because of him that Octavius and Antony are reconciled. They will rivet the alliance by means of Antony's marriage to Caesar's sister. Enobarbus knows automatically that this union is a certain way of making conflict ultimately inevitable.

> you shall find the bond that seems to tie their friendship together will be the very strangler of their amity.
>   (II.vi.7-9)

Octavia is one of Shakespeare's minor triumphs in the play, beautifully placed in relation to the main figures and the tenor of their meaning. Her importance is apt to be overlooked unless her

careful positioning is noted. Her presence gives a symmetrical
form to the main relations of the play. Octavia is the opposite of
Cleopatra as Antony is the opposite of Caesar. She is woman made
the submissive tool of Roman policy where Cleopatra always
strives to make the political subservient to her. (It is the thought
of being led in triumph by Caesar as much as the thought of
Antony's death which finally decides Cleopatra for suicide.)
Where Caesar and Cleopatra are simple and opposite, Octavia—
like Antony—is a focal point for the contraries. There is nothing
in her as a "character-study" to account for the effect her presence has. It is rather that she is transparent to the reality behind
the play and one of its least mistakable mediators. On the occasions when she appears herself, or when mention is made of
her, it is the interfluent life of this reality rather than the personality of its vehicle which fills the scene.

Her first entry is significant. It comes immediately after the
triumvirate and Pompey have made their pact. We have just
heard the following satiric account of Lepidus's behaviour—and
Lepidus, like Octavia, has to stand between the two demi-Atlases:

> *Agrippa.* 'Tis a noble Lepidus.
> *Eno.* A very fine one. O! how he loves Caesar.
> *Agrippa.* Nay, but how dearly he adores Mark Antony.
> *Eno.* Caesar? Why, he's the Jupiter of men!
> *Agrippa.* What's Antony? the god of Jupiter.
> *Eno.* Spake you of Caesar? How, the nonpareil!
> *Agrippa.* O Antony! O thou Arabian bird!
>   (III.ii.6-12)

Then the triumvirate and Octavia come on. Octavia stirs Antony
deeply. But the imagery in which his vision of her is clothed
carries us past the person described to the "varying tide" by which
everything in the play is moved:

> Her tongue will not obey her heart, nor can
> Her heart obey her tongue; the swan's down feather
> That stands upon the swell of the full tide
> And neither way inclines.   (III.ii.47-50)

Octavia never escapes from her position midway between the
contraries that maintain and split the world. With Antony away
in Athens, her brother first falls on Pompey then finds a pretext
to destroy Lepidus. He is now ready to mount his attack on the

last remaining rival, his "competitor in top of all design." Hearing of it, Octavia cries:

> A more unhappy lady,
> If this division chance, ne'er stood between,
> Praying for both parts....
> ...Husband win, win brother,
> Prays and destroys the prayer; no midway
> 'Twixt these extremes at all.   (III.iv.12-20)

Octavia's is the alternative plight to Cleopatra's for womanhood in the play. The choice is merely between alternative methods of destruction—either at one's own hands, or through the agency of the process. The "swan's down feather," like the "vagabond flag," can only swing on the tide until it rots with motion.

Rome is the world of politics and policy. Its supreme term is Octavius Caesar himself. He, like Octavia, must be brought into relation with the pattern which he helps in part to define. Half his significance is lost if he is seen only as a "character." In Octavius's case we have aids external to the play which help towards a clear focus on what Shakespeare intends by him. He falls recognizably into Shakespeare's studies of the "politician"—the series that begins with Richard III and continues down through Edmund.

Octavius is a notable development in the figure which started as a machiavel pure and simple. Shakespeare now betrays no sign of alarm, no hint of revulsion or rejection, almost no trace of emotion in putting him into a story. He is taken completely for granted. He has arrived and he will stay. He is part of the structure of things. He is "Rome." In matters of politics and policy it is obvious that only the politicians count: and politics is one half of life. The politician is a perfectly normal person. Given all his own way he would doubtless bring—as Octavius is certain his triumphs eventually will bring—a "universal peace." To be normal like him, of course, and to enjoy the peace he offers, two conditions are necessary. First, one must sacrifice the other half of life; then, one must be prepared to make complete submission. By the time Shakespeare comes to depict Octavius he has refined away all the accidentals from the portrait—the diabolism, the rhetoric, the elaborate hypocrisy, the perverse glamour: everything but the essential deadliness and inescapability. Octavius

marks an advance on Goneril and Regan. He shares their im-
patience with tavern and brothel. He has no share in the lust
which entraps even them. We might almost doubt whether Octavius has any personal appetite at all, even the lust for power.
His plan to lead Cleopatra in triumph has the appearance of a
desire for personal satisfaction, but it is more likely that it fits
into an impersonal wish on Caesar's part to subdue all things to
Rome. Caesar, of course, is Rome—but a kind of impersonal embodiment. He is more like a cold and universal force than a warm-
blooded man. He is the perfect commissar, invulnerable as no
human being should be. Egypt has no part in his composition.

Caesar has the deceitfulness of the machiavel, but he plays his
cards without any flourish. He can rely on his opponents to undo
themselves: they are more complicated than he. He puts the
deserters from Antony in the van of his own battle:

> Plant those that are revolted in the van,
> That Antony may seem to spend his fury
> Upon himself.   (IV.vi.9-11)

The strength and weakness of those ranged against him constitute Caesar's fifth column. The opposition will rot away or eat
the sword it fights with.

It is in the last act that Egypt and Rome confront each other
singly, the duplicity of Caesar pitted against the duplicity of
Cleopatra. There is no doubt as to who shall survive the contest.
The tension is maintained throughout the fifth act only by the
doubt left in the spectator's mind right up to the end as to which
way Cleopatra will jump: will she accept submission or will she
take her own life? The whole play has prepared us for just this
doubt. In a sense, whichever way the decision goes it is immaterial.
The point of the play is not the decisions taken but the dubieties
and ambivalences from which choice springs—the barren choice
that only hastens its own negation. Rome, from the nature of
things, can admit no compromise. Egypt, equally, can never sub-
mit to its contrary. So Cleopatra kills herself.

Cleopatra has been loved by recent commentators not wisely
but too well. As Caesar impersonates the World, she, of course,
incarnates the Flesh. Part of Shakespeare's sleight of hand in the
play—his trickery with our normal standards and powers of judgment—is to construct an account of the human universe consisting
of only these two terms. There is no suggestion that the dichot-

omy is resolvable: unless we are willing to take the delusions of either party as a resolution, the "universal peace" of Caesar, the Egypt-beyond-the-grave of Antony and Cleopatra in their auto-toxic exaltations before they kill themselves.

Cleopatra is the Flesh, deciduous, opulent, and endlessly renewable:

> she did make defect perfection...
> Age cannot wither her, nor custom stale
> Her infinite variety; other women cloy
> The appetites they feed, but she makes hungry
> Where most she satisfies; for vilest things
> Become themselves in her, that the holy priests
> Bless her when she is riggish.   (II.ii.239-248)

The Flesh is also the female principle. Cleopatra is Eve, and Woman:

> No more but e'en a woman, and commanded
> By such poor passion as the maid that milks
> And does the meanest chares.
>   (IV.xiii.73-75)

She is also Circe:

> Let witchcraft join with beauty, lust with both!   (II.i.22)

Shakespeare gives Cleopatra everything of which he is capable except his final and absolute approval. Cleopatra is not an Octavia, much less a Cordelia. The profusion of rich and hectic colour that surrounds her is the colour of the endless cycle of growth and decay, new greenery on old rottenness, the colour of the passions, the wild flaring of life as it burns itself richly away to death so that love of life and greed for death become indistinguishable:

> there is mettle in death which commits some loving act upon her,
> she hath such a celerity in dying.   (I.ii.152-154)

The strength of the case Shakespeare puts against her is undeniable. The soldiers, and Caesar, and Antony when the consciousness of Rome speaks through him, are right, as far as they go. The strength of the case for her is that it is only Rome that condemns her. And Egypt is a force as universal as Rome—as hot as the other is cold, as inevitably self-renewing as the other is inescapably deadly. And the only appeal that can be made in the

play is from Egypt to Rome, from Rome to Egypt. And neither
of these is final, because between them they have brought down
Antony, the "man of men."

For the tragedy of *Antony and Cleopatra* is, above all, the tragedy of Antony. His human stature is greater than either Cleopatra's or Caesar's. Yet there is no sphere in which he can express
himself except either Rome or Egypt, and to bestride both like a
Colossus and keep his balance is impossible. The opposites play
through Antony and play with him, and finally destroy him. To
Caesar (while Antony is in Egypt, and alive) he is:

> A man who is the abstract of all faults
> That all men follow.   (I.iv.9-10)

To Cleopatra he appears instead a "heavenly mingle":

> Be'st thou sad or merry,
> The violence of either thee becomes,
> So it does no man else.   (I.v.59-61)

When she sees him returning safe from the battlefield she cries:

> O infinite virtue! Com'st thou smiling from
> The world's great snare uncaught?
>   (IV.viii.17-18)

After he is dead she remembers him as a kind of Mars:

> His face was as the heavens, and therein stuck
> A sun and moon, which kept their course, and lighted
> This little O, the earth...
> His legs bestrid the ocean; his rear'd arm
> Crested the world; his voice was propertied
> As all the tuned spheres, and that to friends;
> But when he meant to quail and shake the orb,
> He was as rattling thunder. For his bounty,
> There was no winter in't, an autumn 'twas
> That grew the more by reaping; his delights
> Were dolphin-like, they show'd his back above
> The element they lived in; in his livery
> Walk'd crowns and crownets, realms and islands were
> As plates dropped from his pocket...
>   ...Nature wants stuff
> To vie strange forms with fancy, yet t'imagine
> An Antony were nature's piece 'gainst fancy,
> Condemning shadows quite.   (V.ii.79-99)

This, of course, is again the past catching fire from the urgent needs of the present, flaring in memory and imagination as it never did in actuality. Antony is nothing so unambiguous as this. The most judicious account of him is that of Lepidus when he is replying to Caesar's strictures:

> I must not think there are
> Evils enow to darken all his goodness:
> His faults in him seem as the spots of heaven,
> More fiery by night's blackness; hereditary
> Rather than purchased, what he cannot change
> Than what he chooses.   (I.iv.10-15)

Here the ambiguities of the play's moral universe get their completest expression: faults shine like stars, the heaven is black, the stars are spots. Ambivalence need go no further.

IV

The earlier criticism of *Antony and Cleopatra* tended to stress the downfall of the soldier in the middle-aged infatuate. More recent criticism has seen the play as the epiphany of the soldier in the lover, and the reassurance of all concerned that death is not the end. In the view that has been put forward here neither of these is right. The meaning of *Antony and Cleopatra* is in the Shakespearian "dialectic"—in the deliquescent reality that expresses itself through the contraries.

Antony and Cleopatra swims with glamour. Once we lose sight of the controlling structure of the opposites which holds the play together we are at the mercy of any random selection from its occasions. And occasions abound—moments, opinions, moods, speeches, characters, fragments of situation, forked mountains and blue promontories, imposed upon us with all the force of a "giant power." It is, then, eminently understandable that critics should succumb like Antony or hold aloof like Demetrius and Philo.

The Roman condemnation of the lovers is obviously inadequate. The sentimental reaction in their favour is equally mistaken. There is no so-called "love-romanticism" in the play. The flesh has its glory and passion, its witchery. Love in *Antony and Cleopatra* is both these. The love of Antony and Cleopatra, however, is not asserted as a "final value." The whole tenour of the play, in fact, moves in an opposite direction. Egypt is the Egypt of the biblical glosses: exile from the spirit, thraldom to the flesh-pots, diminution of human kindness. To go further still in senti-mentality and claim that there is a "redemption" motif in Antony and Cleopatra's love is an even more violent error. To the Shake-speare who wrote *King Lear* it would surely smack of blasphemy. The fourth and fifth acts of *Antony and Cleopatra* are not epiph-anies. They are the ends moved to by that process whereby things rot themselves with motion—unhappy and bedizened and sordid, streaked with the mean, the ignoble, the contemptible. Shake-speare may have his plays in which "redemption" is a theme (and I think he has), but *Antony and Cleopatra* is not one of them.

Antony and Cleopatra is an account of things in terms of the World and the Flesh, Rome and Egypt, the two great contraries that maintain and destroy each other, considered apart from any third sphere which might stand over against them. How is it re-lated to the plays of the "great period," the period which comes to an end with *King Lear?*

The clue is given, I think, in the missing third term. *Antony and Cleopatra* is the deliberate construction of a world without a Cordelia, Shakespeare's symbol for a reality that transcends the political and the personal and

> redeems nature from the general curse
> Which twain have brought her to.
> *(King Lear,* IV.vi.211-212)

One must call the construction deliberate, because after *King Lear* there can be no doubt that Shakespeare knew exactly where he was in these matters. Both *Antony and Cleopatra* and *Coriolanus* follow North's Plutarch without benefit of clergy. Both Antony and Coriolanus were cited by the sixteenth-century moralists as notable examples of heathen men who lacked patience—the one committing suicide, the other rebelling against his country. In *Antony and Cleopatra* suicide is the general fate of those who wish to die. Cleopatra gives the audience a conscious reminder of the un-Christian ethos involved:

> All's but naught;
> Patience is sottish, and impatience does
> Become a dog that's mad: then is it sin

> To rush into the secret house of death
> Ere death dare come to us?
> (IV.xiii.78-82)

The Christian world-view in Shakespeare's time turned round a number of conceptions which were covered by the Elizabethans in their examination of the meanings of "Nature." The theme of "Nature" runs through the whole of *Macbeth, King Lear,* and *Timon.* Its absence from *Antony and Cleopatra* suggests Shakespeare's satisfaction that for him the theme is exhausted. He is inwardly free now to look at a classical story, deliberately excise the Christian core of his thought, and make up his account of what then remains over.

This explains the effect, I think, of *Antony and Cleopatra.* Freedom from the compulsive theme of the Natures, the conscious security gained from having given it final expression, enabled Shakespeare to handle something new and something which was bound to be intrinsically simpler. Part of the energy absorbed in grappling with theme now bestows itself on technique. *Antony and Cleopatra* gives the impression of being a technical *tour de force* which Shakespeare enjoyed for its own sake.

The excision also explains, I think, the tone of the play—the sense of ripe-rottenness and hopelessness, the vision of self-destruction, the feeling of strenuous frustration and fevered futility, that which finds its greatest expression in Antony's speech before he gives himself his death-blow:

> Now
> All length is torture; since the torch is out,
> Lie down and stray no further. Now all labour
> Mars what it does; yea, very force entangles
> Itself with strength; seal then, and all is done.
> (IV.xii.45-49)

The excision, finally, explains what might be regarded as a diminution of scope in *Antony and Cleopatra.* (We are, of course, only comparing Shakespeare with himself.) The theme of Rome and Egypt, however, is simpler than the theme of "Nature," the trick of using the contraries (again, for Shakespeare) relatively an easy way of organizing the universe. It is unusual, at any rate, for Shakespeare to rely on one trick so completely as he seems to do in *Antony and Cleopatra.* At times we are almost tempted to believe he has fallen a victim of habitual mannerism.

One last comment might be made. We referred at the beginning of this chapter to Shakespeare's surprising capacity for self-renewal. *Antony and Cleopatra* is not the aftermath of Lear in any pejorative sense. There is something in it that is new and exciting and profound. Shakespeare remained still the youngest as the greatest of his contemporaries. In *Antony and Cleopatra* he is making his own adjustments to the new Jacobean tastes. The play is Shakespeare's study of Mars and Venus—the presiding deities of Baroque society, painted for us again and again on the canvasses of his time. It shows us Virtue, the root of the heroic in man, turned merely into *virtu,* the warrior's art, and both of them ensnared in the world, very force entangling itself with strength. It depicts the "man of men" soldiering for a cynical Rome or whoring on furlough in a reckless Egypt. It is the tragedy of the destruction of man, the creative spirit, in perverse war and insensate love—the two complementary and opposed halves of a discreating society.

For more obvious, if less great manifestations of the same discreating society, interested almost exclusively in love and war (and these both more narrowly conceived and more over-valued emotionally than they ever are by Shakespeare) we must turn to Beaumont.

Antony and Cleopatra

by John Holloway

Those who believe, like Mr. Bethell, that "in *Antony and Cleopatra*, Shakespeare returns to the old problem: what are the positive bases of the good life? He finds them in the affections, and in the affections as rooted deep in the sensual nature"; or like Professor Wilson Knight, that "to understand the play aright we must be prepared to see...Cleopatra as love herself,"[1] will think it perverse to begin a discussion of this play by quoting Shakespeare's Sonnet 129:

> The expense of spirit in a waste of shame
> Is lust in action; and till action, lust
> Is perjur'd, murd'rous, bloody, full of blame,
> Savage, extreme, rude, cruel, not to trust;
> Enjoyed no sooner but despised straight;
> Past reason hunted, and, no sooner had,
> Past reason hated, as a swallowed bait,
> On purpose laid to make the taker mad—
> Mad in pursuit, and in possession so;
> Had, having, and in quest to have, extreme;
> A bliss in proof, and prov'd, a very woe;
> Before, a joy propos'd; behind, a dream.
>   All this the world well knows; yet none knows well
>   To shun the heaven that leads men to this hell.

"*Antony and Cleopatra.*" From *The Story of the Night: Studies in Shakespeare's Major Tragedies,* by John Holloway (London: Routledge & Kegan Paul Ltd., 1961), pp. 99-120. Copyright © 1961 by John Holloway. Reprinted by permission of the publisher.

[1]S. L. Bethell, *Shakespeare and the Popular Dramatic Tradition* (1930), p. 130; G. W. Knight, *The Imperial Theme* (1951 ed.), p. 324. Cf. p. 304: "Cleopatra is all womankind, therefore all romantic vision, the origin of love, the origin of life."

Yet however much it may be thought perverse to quote a sonnet on lust in the context of these lovers, it cannot be denied that at the very outset of the play Shakespeare puts before his audience, as emphatically as he can, the issue of whether the spectacle before them is one of love or of lust. Philo, in his first speech, says that Antony's heart

>   is become the bellows and the fan
>   To cool a gipsy's *lust.*

The main characters enter, and Cleopatra's first words are: "If it be *love indeed,* tell me how much."

Whether Antony and Cleopatra lust, or love, or something of both, is probably a matter on which complete agreement cannot be expected. Men use these words as they are guided not only by their sense of value, but also by their experience of life; both of these are liable to much variation, and the critic may find that opportunities for augmenting the second are, in his case, slight, past or unwelcome. Sonnet 129 helps the reader of *Antony and Cleopatra* for two reasons. First it shows Shakespeare speaking of the experience of lust in a very remarkable way. Ferocious as is his condemnation of it in the earlier lines of the poem, and sorrowful as is his portrait of what follows after it is sated, for all that he calls it nothing less than "a *bliss* in proof." The last line is more emphatic still. Whether it refers to what precedes lust, or to the actual satisfying of lust, or to both at once, it is still nothing short of a "heaven." It is still to be described by no less a word than that which Cleopatra employs at the very climax of the play:

>   ...that kiss
>   Which is my Heaven to have.
>   (V.ii.300)

It is clear that "lust," in this sonnet, means something quite different from what is occasionally termed "cocktail sex."

Most critics have tried (or perhaps "struggled" is the word) to express how the relation between Antony and Cleopatra cannot be seen simply. Mr. Traversi, who said that from one point of view the play was Shakespeare's supreme expression of "love as *value,*" also said that to see it as depicting a "senseless surrender to passion" was defensible. Professor L. C. Knights refers to an "absolute value" in the sense of heightened life and energy infused by Shakespeare into the love story, but also suggests that the energy is in Antony's own case, merely "galvanized," and that "the sense of potentiality in life's untutored energies" is discarded or condemned. (Whether these contradictory assertions are adequately reconciled in his description is a question which need not be pursued.) Professor Danby, starting as it were from the opposite end, writes: *"Antony and Cleopatra* is an account of things in terms of the World and the Flesh, Rome and Egypt, the two great contraries that maintain and destroy each other, considered apart from any third sphere that might stand over against them."[2] But for Professor Danby, it transpires, the Flesh is more than some might think: it "has its glory and passion, its witchery. Love in *Antony and Cleopatra* is both these."

If readers find, rightly, that there is something both vague and strained about all these accounts, perhaps that is because a remarkable fact about the bond between the lovers has been consistently overlooked. Whether the bond in question is love, or passion, or both, it is neither of these which the lovers themselves mainly bring to light when they speak of each other or of what is between them. It is a certain third thing, which will prove to operate in association with these, although in essence it remains quite distinct from them.

This "third thing" transpires from the very start. Cleopatra's first words, admittedly, were "if it be love indeed, tell me how much." But insofar as Antony does tell her, it is a very particular kind of "how much" that he stresses:

> The *nobleness* of life
> Is to do thus [embracing], when such a mutual pair
> And such a twain can do 't, in which *I bind*
> *On pain of punishment, the world to weet*
> We stand up *peerless*. (I.i.36)

Antony does not always talk so ("I' th' East my *pleasure* lies"); but this is the attitude which re-emerges at Cleopatra's death. His pointed "I come, my queen" leads into a vision of their reunion after death; yet surely, for those who weigh it, this vision is a remarkable one:

> Where souls do couch on flowers, we'll hand in hand,
> and *with our spritely port make the ghosts gaze.*
> Dido and her Aeneas shall want troops
> And *all the haunt be ours.* (IV.xiv.51)

[2] J. Danby, *Poets on Fortune's Hill* (1952), p. 149.

The peerless pair are not re-united in the intimacy of their love
for each other, but are to be the cynosure of the world to come, as
they have been of this one. Antony immediately goes on to see in
Cleopatra herself exactly what he had seen in his love with her

> I, that with my sword
> Quarter'd the world, and o'er green Neptune's back
> With ships made cities, condemn myself to lack
> The courage of a woman; less *noble* mind
> Than she which by her death our Caesar tells
> "I am conqueror of myself."   (IV.xiv.57)

This sense of having the role of greatness to live up to, runs
throughout the play. It shows at Antony's meeting with Octavius
and Lepidus (see the passage quoted on p. 71), it shows in his
attitude to Octavia:

> Gentle Octavia,
> Let your best love draw to that point which seeks
> Best to preserve it. If I lose mine *honour*
> I lose myself; better I were not yours
> Than yours so branchless.   (III.iv.20)

It shows in his magnanimity to the renegade Enobarbus. It is
sustained (for it is, one must remember, an outward greatness,
the bounteous lordliness of a colossus of public life, one who
dominates the stage of history) in his feasting, his generosity,
his valour and spiritedness in the last campaign against Caesar;
and it is confirmed in the words of the soothsayer:

> Thy daemon, that thy spirit which keeps thee, is
> Noble, courageous, high, unmatchable. ...
>   (II.iii.20)

That Antony's greatness is subject to moods of indulgence, irre-
sponsibility and depression, and that it is far from anything
which easily wins the name of greatness without reserve, is not to
the point. But it is very much to the point to notice how, at an
early stage in the play, it is a greatness which is one with his incomparable *physical* resilience:

> at thy heel
> Did famine follow; whom thou fought'st against,
> Though daintily brought up, with patience more
> Than savages could suffer. Thou didst drink

> The stale of horses and the gilded puddle
> Which beasts would cough at...
>   ...And all this—
> It wounds thine *honour* that I speak it now—
> Was borne so like a soldier that thy cheek
> So much as lanked not.   (I.iv.58)

Before this, Antony has given to the younger Pompey just such praise as he merits himself:

>   who, high in name and power,
> Higher than both in *blood and life,* stands up
> For the main soldier.   (I.ii.183)

Yet if Antony, at the moment of disaster and crisis, dwells less on love than on his and his queen's nobility—so does she. It is easy to allow our own familiar ideas to play too freely in our minds, and make us see Cleopatra's delight in Antony's greatness as going merely with a woman's private affection and devotion towards her mate; but when she says:

> His face was as the heav'ns...
> His legs bestrid the ocean; his rear'd arm
> Crested the world. His voice was propertied
> As all the tuned spheres....   (V.ii.79)

Dolabella, at once paying her what he sees as the acceptable compliment, guides us to how she glories in Antony's glory as counterpart to her own:

> Your loss is, *as yourself, great:* and you bear it
> As *answering* to the weight.   (V.ii.101)

What Cleopatra sees as calling her to commit suicide is not her love and her loss; but nobility:

>   Good sirs, take heart.
> We'll bury him; and then, what's *brave,* what's *noble,*
> Let's do it after the high Roman fashion,
> And *make earth proud to take us.*   (IV.xv.85)

When she comes to die ("most *noble* Empress," Dolabella has just called her), it is *"Noble* Charmian" who means to die with her. "What poor an instrument/ May do a *noble* deed" she says when the asps are brought in (V.ii.235); and "Methinks I hear/

Antony call. I see him rouse himself/ To praise my *noble* act" she goes on. Yet is this not to imagine a lovers' reunion of a very distinctive kind? The distinctiveness is confirmed a moment later when, seeing Iras dying before her, she imagines her arriving first in the Elysian fields, and receiving from Antony "that kiss/ Which is my heaven to have." It is clear that Antony would not kiss Iras as if she were the woman he loved: he would kiss her as a public act of recognition and high praise. Plainest of all, perhaps, is what follows the words: "Husband, I come":

> Now to that name my *courage* prove my title   (V.ii.286)

The Eastern star is a fit bride for the triple pillar of the world. Her title to the honour, though, is not the completeness of her love: it is her own honour—her courage, greatness of spirit, nobility, stressed once again in the words which follow: "I am fire and air; my other elements/I give to *baser* life."

This antithesis between noble and base is a constant one:

> Since Cleopatra died
> I have lived in such dishonour that the gods
> Detest my baseness...

is Antony's expression of it (IX.xiv.55). Cleopatra's is her "This proves me base" (V.ii.298) when she thinks that Iras will be first to meet Antony. To be able only to say in general terms that the love of these lovers is less than love in the fullest, or passion in the merest sense, was to say little. But here is the third term upon which Shakespeare depends to qualify the other two: that third quality of mind or emotion which exalts passion, or renders love less than itself, in a definite and distinctive way. Both the lovers find, in their love, the manifestation and continuance of their own greatness, their glory as people made on a larger and grander scale than average life. This is the kind of nobility which it has (one genuinely noble, in its way, though it has nothing of the more inward nobility of Kent or Hermione); and this is what gives it its quality of dramatized exaltation, its eloquence, its superb if also savage egotism. There is more to recognize. The love of Antony and Cleopatra is not related to their greatness as its mere effect. It is not only effect, it is also cause: it is the source of their greatness. As other lines of life are closed to them, the lovers find more and more, each in the other, an incomparable model of nobility and spirit, one which it is their over-riding thought to emulate.

Yet if Antony and Cleopatra mutually inspire each other with a spectacle of greatness, the play could not be more different than it is from, say, *Bérénice:* there is nothing remote or self-denying in their exaltation. This is because, throughout the play, Shakespeare sees the greatness of both as one with their intense and exuberant physical energy; and it seems to be part of his sense of the whole situation, that exuberance of this order actually issues, in its turn, from sexuality itself in the full tide of its fulfilment. Cleopatra's vitality—"Age cannot wither her, nor custom stale/ Her infinite variety" (II.iii.239)—is a match for Antony's as hardened campaigner; and it is a vitality that inevitably takes the form of an irresistible sexual fascination and life:

> I saw her once
> Hop forty paces through the public street;
> And having lost her breath, she spoke, and panted,
> That she did make defect perfection,
> And, *breathless, pow'r breathed forth.*

(II.iii.232)

Whatever she does, her spirits and energy turn always one way; whether it is hanging a dead fish on Antony's rod as he fishes, out drinking him, dressing him in her own clothes as he lies in drunken sleep, or roystering in disguise with him at night. What is more, this is exactly how he sees her. Planning this night-time prank, Antony makes it plain that for him, it is Cleopatra's vitality that makes her sexually irresistible; and that it does so with a nuance that leaves her an object of wondering admiration. The sequence, "Every passion...fair...admir'd," in the following lines (they come in the opening moments of the play, and lay down how we are to see the rest of it) set this beyond doubt:

> ...queen...
> Whom everything becomes—to chide, to laugh,
> To weep; whose every passion fully strives
> To make itself in thee fair and admired.
> No messenger but thine, and all alone
> Tonight we'll wander through the streets. ...

(I.i.48)

On the other hand, Cleopatra's image of Antony is of one whose inexhaustible vitality is physical and sexual through and through:

> For his bounty,
> There was no winter in 't; an autumn 'twas

> That grew the more by reaping. His delights
> Were dolphin-like: they showed his back above
> The element they lived in.[3]   (V.ii.86)

The third term, which explains exactly how Antony and Cleopatra do more than lust, if they do less than love, is thus their
glory. Each finds in the other, and sustains in himself, a greatness
which is inseparable from an incomparable physical energy; and
in each, and in each's image of the other, this physical energy is an
exuberant embodiment of their attraction as lovers. Nobility is a
modulation of vitality, and that of sexuality. With beautiful completeness and detail (and, some will find, with a rewarding knowledge of life) Shakespeare has drawn together, as extreme links of
one continuous chain

> O, see, my women,
> The crown o' th' earth doth melt. My lord!
> O, wither'd is the garland of the war...
>   (IV.xv.62)

and

>   the bellows and the fan
> To cool a gipsy's lust.   (I.i.9)

The highest and lowest, the most exalted and the base, in the end
were one.

At something like this point many discussions of this play, as of
others, cease; their authors supposing, presumably, that the substance of the work has been dealt with. What has been dealt with
so far, however, is the mere basic recipe for a situation, or merely
those potential linkages and associations in human response,
emotion and conduct which the work brings into play (its "values,"
some would say):—but not the play that it makes with them through
its unfolding action: what *transpires,* we could say, not what is
transacted. In this latter respect *Antony and Cleopatra* is especially
interesting. It arrives at a very remarkable kind of resolution—
one which it is a *tour de force* on Shakespeare's part to achieve—
and it does so through a rhythm of local progression which
(though some have found it loose or confusing) is profoundly
right for its idea and structure as a whole.

---

[3]The idea of Antony's nobility is present here too, however, in the reference
to the dolphin, the king of sea-creatures.

Once again, a clue may perhaps be found in Sonnet 129. This sonnet reminds us that lust, and (let us pass over experience in silence) innumerable passages in Elizabethan literature remind us that love, is a constant and vehement oscillation, an unbroken to-and-fro between positive and negative, mood and mood. So is *Antony and Cleopatra*. So, to a certain extent, is every narrative; but to notice this in *Antony and Cleopatra* is not to place an arbitrary stress, in this one case, on what could be stressed in every case. This oscillation governs the very substance of the play. "Give me some music...Let it alone! Let's to billiards...I'll none now. Give me mine angle—we'll to the river" (II.v.1-10) says Cleopatra while Antony is away. The messenger enters, and even before he delivers his message, she calls him a villain, gives him gold, then threatens to melt it and pour it down his throat. When she hears his news, she drives him away, calls him back, dismisses him, calls him again, dismisses him again, then sends after him to hear more. Her final thought is of Antony, and is in just the same vein: "Let him for ever go—let him not, Charmian" (II.v.115). She is as inconstant when Antony is at hand as when he is not: "If you find him sad/ Say I am dancing; if in mirth, report/ That I am sudden sick..." (I.iii.3)

Antony is the same, both as she describes him when he says, "He was disposed to mirth; but on the sudden/ A Roman thought hath struck him" (I.ii.79); and, more substantially, in whole contrasting episodes: for example when, infatuated with Cleopatra's physical presence (I.i), he refuses to hear the ambassadors from Rome, in contrast with the later episode where he searchingly questions the same messenger, and concludes: "I must from this enchanting queen break off" (I.ii.125). A line earlier he confirms the point: "The present pleasure,/ By revolution low'ring, does become/ The opposite of itself." Act II scene iii epitomizes the contrast. It opens with Antony bidding goodnight to Octavia just after his betrothal to her, and the appearance, anyhow, of sincerity is decisive:

> My Octavia,
> Read not my blemishes in the world's report.
> I have not kept my square; but that to come
> Shall all be done by th' rule.   (II.iii.4)

The soothsayer enters; his warning to Antony merely echoes a truth already in the hearer's mind; and within twenty lines:

> I will to Egypt;
> And though I make this marriage for my peace,
> I' the' East my pleasure lies.

The other side of Antony's nature is awake.
  Later in the play, Antony reverts once more:

> Ha!
> Have I my pillow left unpress'd in Rome,
> Forborne the getting of a lawful race,
> And by a gem of women, to be abus'd
> By one that looks on feeders?
>   (III.xiii.105)

This is what Antony says to Cleopatra when he finds her with
Thyreus. In the closing scenes "Antony/ Is valiant and dejected"
says Scarus (IV.xii.6); and in the last stages of the campaign,
almost unbalanced oscillation between shrewdness and folly,
hopefulness and despair, love and hate, need no illustration. This
constant oscillation, finally, is also symbolized in the river of
Egypt itself:

> *Antony.* ...The higher Nilus swells
>   The more it promises; as it ebbs, the seedsman
>   Upon the slime and ooze scatters his grain,
>   And shortly comes to harvest   (II.vii.20)

and gives substance to some of the most memorable images in
the play:

> This common body,
> Like to a vagabond flag upon the stream,
> Goes to and back, lackeying the varying tide,
> To rot itself with motion.   (I.iv.44)

> Her tongue will not obey her heart, nor can
> Her heart inform her tongue—the swan's down feather,
> That stands upon the swell at the full of tide,
> And neither way inclines.   (III.ii.48)

—this kind of stability is really the quintessence of vacillation.
  The world of politics in this play is a world of flux as well. That
this is true of the constant to-and-fro between Rome and Egypt,
the stages where Antony plays as general and as lover, needs no
confirmation; in its wide and hurried movement from place to
place, *Antony and Cleopatra* probably stands by itself among all

Shakespeare's works. The same movement shows in the fortunes of war, and of the diplomacy that precedes the war. Antony's position is weakening all the time; yet it does so not through steady decline, but through a constant alternation of failure and comparative success. More intimately, in a sense, there is a constant oscillation in the balance of moral evaluation. All the time, we are invited to think now better and now worse of the scene before us; this is equally true of public life and of private. At their first meeting (at II.ii.27; the passage requires study in full) Caesar and Antony are distrustful of each other and careful not to lose face, but it would be crude to accept Enobarbus's sceptical comment without having in mind that the whole scene is a judgment, in its turn, upon the comment. His

> ...if you borrow one another's love for the instant, you may, when you hear no more words of Pompey, return it again...

is something that Maecenas has already set in a more sympathetic light:

> If it might please you to enforce no further
> The griefs between you— to forget them quite
> Were to remember that the present need
> Speaks to atone you.   (II.ii.103)

When Antony reproves Enobarbus with: "Thou art a soldier only. Speak no more" (II.ii.112), he is not simply excluding an honest soldier from a dishonest manoeuvre. The honesty is a kind of impercipience, the manoeuvring honest within its limits. One is likely to be told that this is naïve; but perhaps the naïveté comes in being confident of that. In fact Antony is held back by a sense of his own glory, Caesar by a sense of what is feasible; yet both speak with a note of sincerity against which Enobarbus's words have only limited weight:

> *Antony.* As nearly as I may,
>   I'll play the penitent to you; but mine honesty
>   Shall not make poor my greatness...
>   For which myself, the ignorant motive, do
>   So far ask pardon as befits mine honour
>   To stoop in such a case.   (II.ii.95)
> *Caesar.* It cannot be
>   We shall remain in friendship, our conditions
>   So diff'ring in their acts. Yet if I knew

> What hoop should hold us stanch, from edge to edge
> O' th' world, I would pursue it.   (II.ii.116)

Similarly with the marriage of Antony to Octavia. Mr. Traversi's reiterated "shameful proceeding," "supremely cynical suggestion," "most dishonorable project," "cynical transaction"[4] in this connection suggest a distaste against which lucidity fights a losing battle. A marriage to cement an alliance need have nothing cynical, shameful or dishonourable about it; and the play gives no reason whatever to suppose that the "helpless sister Octavia" either was helpless in respect of her devoted brother (Shakespeare seems to follow Plutarch here),[5] or would have wished to help herself in any way other than by furthering his wishes. Attitudes like this may have become obsolete, but they are neither incomprehensible nor unattractive.

> *Menas.* Then is Caesar and he [Antony] for ever knit together.
> *Enobarbus.* If I were bound to divine of this unity, I would not
>   prophesy so.
> *Menas.* I think the policy of that purpose made more in the
>   marriage than the love of the parties.
> *Enobarbus.* I think so too. But you shall find the band that seems
>   to tie their friendship together will be the very strangler of
>   their amity.   (II.vi.111)

There is nothing cynical in this, and if there is something un-realistic, it is balanced by what Caesar says later: instead of Enobarbus's dismissal, we have genuine awareness of a danger, envisaged openly and humanely:

> Most noble Antony,
> Let not the piece of virtue which is set
> Betwixt us as the cement of our love
> To keep it builded be the ram to batter
> The fortress of it; for better might we
> Have loved without this mean, if on both parts
> This be not cherished.   (III.ii.27)

Plutarch's comment again has its relevance: "everybody concurred in promoting this new alliance, fully expecting that...all would be kept in the safe and happy course of friendship." Later on in Plutarch's account, Octavia calls herself "the most fortunate woman on earth...wife and sister of the two great commanders."

---

[4]*An Approach to Shakespeare*, pp. 244-45.

[5]Plutarch, *Life of Antony*.

These attitudes are nearer to Shakespeare's by far than those of today.

The alternations of the play continue. Caesar and Antony, at their leave-taking, plainly seem sincere in their wish for amity and affection for Octavia; but in the whispered conversation of Enobarbus and Agrippa which follows, we are at once reminded to watch those in the game for power with an eye for their guile. Act III scene iv, and Act III scene vi, an exactly matched pair of scenes, bring out both the justice, and the petulant over-touchiness, of each commander's sense that he has been wronged by the other. Caesar's speeches at the death of Antony (V.ii.35) and Cleopatra (V.ii.350) cannot be cynically taken; both unmistakably justify Agrippa's "Caesar is touched." Yet in each, the speaker's sense of his own position and dignity is delicately but inescapably sustained.

That the fluctuations of the war are fluctuations within an over-riding direction needs no argument. But this is the medium of, and subordinate to, the play's central concern. The panorama of the Civil War, of Roman politics, is the mere occasion and reflection of the developing ordeal of Antony and Cleopatra. In this matter, Shakespeare is once again following Plutarch, who begins his summing-up of the career of Antony by saying that he was among "great examples of the vicissitudes of Fortune"; by which Plutarch did not mean the constant and directionless fluctuations of life, but the great reversals which bring men from the summit of fortune to its nadir.

Shakespeare is writing with just such an event in mind; and he gives it the emphasis which has been observed in the earlier tragedies. Here, as before, the protagonists begin not merely at the height of Fortune, but as the cynosure and exemplar of all. Antony is "the triple pillar of the world" (I.i.12), and

> The demi-Atlas of this earth, the arm
> And burgonet of men.   (I.v.23)

Enobarbus's account of Cleopatra on the barge culminates in the idea that she was in the most literal sense the object of everyone's gaze, the ceremonial figure in the centre of the stage. But so (except for her) was Antony:

> The city cast
> Her people out upon her; *and Antony*
> *Enthron'd i' th' market-place,* did sit alone

> Whistling to th' air; which, but for vacancy,
> Had gone to gaze on Cleopatra too,
> And made a gap in nature.   (II.iii.217)

Yet at once, the play instructs its audience to watch for the beginning of a change. "You have seen and prov'd a fairer former fortune/ Than that which is to approach," says the soothsayer to Charmian (I.ii.32); "Ten thousand harms, more than the ills I know,/ My idleness doth hatch" (I.ii.126) is Antony's statement of it (I.ii.126); or again "Much is breeding/ Which, like the courser's hair, hath yet but life/ And not a serpent's poison." (I.ii.186.) Accept these as guides, and one cannot but begin to trace a now familiar kind of movement. Despite all differences of situation or character, the resemblance is plain, at a radical level, with the careers of Hamlet, Othello, Macbeth and Lear.

Antony and Cleopatra both estrange themselves from the environment they grandiosely dominate. Antony's curse on the world of his public life:

> Let Rome in Tiber melt, and the wide arch
> Of the rang'd empire fall! Here is my space. ...
>   (I.i.33)

is something which Cleopatra exactly parallels for hers. (The lines have a special prominence at the end of Act I.)

> Get me ink and paper.
> He shall have every day a several greeting,
> Or I'll *unpeople Egypt*.

Cleopatra in her career of malediction pursues a course reminiscent of Lear: moving from the local to the general, from country to cosmos, from "Sink Rome, and their tongues rot/ That speak against us!" (III.vii.15) to "O sun, Burn the great sphere thou mov'st in! Darkling stand/ The varying shore o' th' world" (IV.xv.9). Antony confirms his status as a gigantic outlaw among mankind by his treatment of Thyreus. The ill-treatment of a messenger is as much a conventionalized act of decisive self-condemnation as Lear's division of the kingdom; and Antony himself, while his position is still relatively undamaged (or at least, still in question or in the balance) reminds the audience of the status of what later on he is to do:

> *Antony.* Well, what worst?
> *Messenger.* The nature of bad news infects the teller.
> *Antony.* When it concerns the fool or coward. On!
> Things that are past are done with me. 'Tis thus:
> Who tells me true, though in his tale lie death,
> I hear him as he flattered. ...
> Speak to me home; mince not the general tongue.
>   (I.ii.91)

This messenger is one of Antony's servants while Thyreus is one of Caesar's, but that makes the parallel only the more telling; and Cleopatra's ill-treatment of the messenger bringing news of Antony's marriage is plainly part of the same carefully-pointed sequence of events.

Macbeth cuts himself off from Duncan and Banquo: the Doctor, and those who flee to the English army, cut themselves off from him. Lear rejects Cordelia and Kent, and receives the like at the hands of Regan and Goneril. To begin with, Antony is isolated and alienated of his own choice. He dismisses the concerns of the Empire, and when we see him (III.iv) sending away Octavia, we know his ulterior motive for doing so. But things do not end as they begun. The words of Canidius make clear what is happening: "To Caesar will I render/ My legions and my horse; six kings already/ Show me the way of yielding" (III.x.33): and the movement is elevated to the plane of the symbolic:

> *Second Soldier.* Hark!
> *Third Soldier.* Music i' th' air.
> *Fourth Soldier.* Under the earth.
> *Third Soldier.* It signs well, does it not?
> *Fourth Soldier.* No.
> *Third Soldier.* Peace, I say!
>   What should this mean?
> *Second Soldier.* 'Tis the god Hercules, whom Antony lov'd,
>   Now leaves him.   (IV.iii.13)

Hercules' example is followed by the man whom Antony most loved, Enobarbus (IV.v); and in a sense by Eros, who refuses (though out of devotion) to do Antony the last service of killing him. Until the death of Antony, no one can significantly desert Cleopatra; but as soon as she is left unsupported, she is first deceived by Proculeius, the one man whom Antony advised her to trust (V.ii.35; cf. IV.xv.48), and then by Seleucus her eunuch (V.ii.144).

Cleopatra, driven to the refuge of her monument and then snared in it, makes a spectacle a little like that of a creature being hunted; and the same idea is clearly worked into the text as an image of the last days of Antony. The word "hunted" is in fact used fairly early on:

> Caesar must think
> When one so great begins to rage, he's *hunted*
> *Even to falling. Give him no breath* but now
> Make boot of his distraction.   (IV.i.6)

Othello driven to his utmost sea-mark, or Macbeth or Gloucester tied like a bear to the stake, have their parallel in his own predicament:

> Unarm, Eros; the long day's task is done,
> And we must sleep...So it must be, for now
> All length is torture. Since the torch is out.
> Lie down, and stray no further. (IV.xiv.35)

The ordeal of Antony is a hunt, and ends as a hunt ends.

Charmian, at one point in the play, invites the audience to see Antony's career just as Plutarch did, as a great example of the vicissitude of Fortune:

> The soul and body rive not more in parting
> Than *greatness going off.*   (IV.xiii.5)

But if Antony may justly say, through the long-drawn-out "agony" (in the strict sense), "the shirt of Nessus is upon me" (IV.xii.43), there is more to this ordeal than this brings out. Or rather, there is a response in him to that ordeal, for which again the clue is in Plutarch: "It was his character in calamities to be better than at any other time. Antony in misfortune was most nearly a virtuous man." Caesar's tribute to how Antony rose above misfortune in his early campaigns has already been quoted (p. 65). This heightened nobility as misfortune gathers about him is plain, and sometimes febrilely over-plain, in his final moments of valour:

> I would they'd fight i' th' fire or i' th' air;
> We'd fight there too.   (IV.x.3)

But it would be wholly false to see this side of Antony, in the closing phase of the drama, as self-discrediting. There is nothing self-discrediting in his forgiveness and generosity for Enobarbus:

> Go, Eros, send his treasure after; do it;
> Detain no jot, I charge thee. Write to him —
> I will subscribe — gentle adieus and greetings;
> Say that I wish he never more find cause
> To change a master. O, my fortunes have
> Corrupted honest men. Dispatch. Enobarbus!
>
> (IV.v.12)

Moreover a new note is heard. Here Antony is speaking with the simplicity and directness not of a public figure, but of a man whose inner life has been touched; and later, his dying words, in spite of what they say, are simple and sincere:

> The miserable change now at my end
> Lament nor sorrow at; but please your thoughts
> In feeding them with those my former fortunes
> Wherein I liv'd the greatest prince o' th' world,
> The noblest; and do now not basely die,
> Not cowardly put off my helmet to
> My countryman — a Roman by a Roman
> Valiantly vanquish'd. Now my spirit is going
> I can no more.[6]   (IV.xv.51)

This is not empty boasting, partly because it is the simple truth that Antony was the greatest and noblest prince in the world, but chiefly because of the tone; in which, more than in his challenging Caesar to single combat (though that too plays its clearly qualified part), we should see something of how Antony was at his best in calamity. It does so, one might say, through indicating that a part of that "best" was for him to take on a "baseness" more significantly the opposite of his valour, his greatness, than the baseness which he fears (and by fits succumbs to). Just as in the retreat from Modena the greatness of the general showed in his readiness to drink filth and eat the bark of trees, so now, along

---

[6]The sense of the passage may be obscure in quotation. "A Roman by a Roman/ valiantly vanquished" is in contrast to what has gone before, and "Roman" perhaps refers both times to Antony himself. Cf. IV.xiv.61-62.

with Antony's exaltation in the face of disaster, there begins to come into the play a new sense of his basic and essential humanity.

> I here importune death awhile, until
> Of many thousand kisses *the poor last*
> I lay upon thy lips.   (IV.xv.19)

This is a "nobleness of life" which hints at a new inwardness and depth; in which, perhaps, many readers today will see, for the first time in Antony, something which is of the spirit not the *persona,* and which they are really willing to call nobility.

"Begins to come into the play," and begins only, however. Shakespeare's sense of what such a nature as Antony's, or Cleopatra's, will do when stretched to breaking-point is complex and complete, but he husbands his resources. He sees both the central characters as impelled into conduct which is sometimes exalted and sometimes abject (Antony's railing at the queen, her several attempts to make terms with Caesar, and finally her subterfuge for keeping back her treasure); and he also sees both as partially divested of the trappings of greatness, because their essential being as humans, their innermost condition of "unaccommodated man," begins in calamity to transpire. But this final turn of the situation he merely hints at with Antony, because he saves its full development for Cleopatra.

Cleopatra's death-scene is the anti-type of Enobarbus's picture of her in all her splendour:

> Now, Charmian!
> Show me, my woman, like a queen. Go fetch
> My best attires. *I am again for Cydnus*
> To meet Mark Antony. ...
> Give me my robe, put on my crown; I have
> Immortal longings in me....   (V.ii.226,278)

The exaltation of the scene, as a moment of supreme greatness, is also made plain in words which gain part of their force from their echo of Antony (the passage was quoted on p. 76):

> I am fire and air; my other elements
> I give to baser life.   (V.ii.287)

But if it is such a moment, the supreme greatness is also to do the one thing left to do in a hopeless, helpless case. "Bravest at the last," Caesar says; but it is bravery with a new quality, less "brave" in the Elizabethan sense, more poignant. The quite new note of a private and personal distress, when Antony calls her down from the monument:

> I dare not, dear.
> Dear my lord, pardon! *I dare not,*
> *Lest I be taken ...*   (IV.xv.21)

leads into her new picture of herself after she has swooned. The great queen begins to be one with women at the other extreme of humanity:

> No more but e'en a woman, and commanded
> By such poor passion as the maid that milks
> And does the meanest chores.   (IV.xv.73)

This new idea of Cleopatra is sustained, immediately before her death, in the scene of her homely conversation with the "simple countryman" who brings the asps; and (fused with its antithesis) continues in Charmian's

> Now boast thee, death, in thy possession lies
> A *lass* unparalleled.   (V.ii.313)

Shakespeare's picture of Cleopatra as "no more but e'en a woman" was also prepared for in other ways. It seems likely that the celebrated lines:

> Do you not see my baby at my breast
> That sucks the nurse asleep?
>   (V.ii.307)

resume the image which Cleopatra has already drawn when she envisaged her death at the beginning of the scene: and offers us reason, perhaps, for accepting the well-known emendation:

> it is great
> To do that thing that ends all other deeds,
> Which shackles accidents and bolts up change,
> Which sleeps, and never palates more the *dug,*
> The beggar's *nurse,* and Caesar's.   (V.ii.4)

Death is a nurse, and at the end of the day she does not feed the child any longer, because she falls asleep.

"The beggar's nurse and Caesar's." A moment later, Cleopatra uses the antithesis again: "If your master/ Would have a queen his beggar..." (V.ii.15). "Beggar" goes with another strand in the converging pattern of suggestion. As the play closes, the Cleopatra who chats with the countryman and dresses in her finery, becomes (one might put it) a gipsy in a new sense, and with a deeper meaning. The idea of dying an outcast's death has already been set in the audience's mind through Enobarbus's resolution to

> go seek
> Some ditch wherein to die; the foul'st best fits
> My latter part of life.   (IV.vi.37)

and also through Cleopatra's curse upon herself, her children, and her people if it is true that she is cold-hearted:

> Ah, dear, if it be so
> From my cold heart let heaven engender hail....
> Till by degrees the memory of my womb
> Together with my brave Egyptians all,
> By the discandying of this pelleted storm,
> Lie graveless, till the flies and gnats of Nile
> Have buried them for prey.   (III.xiii.158)

(which Mr. Traversi, in one of his more remarkable *trouvailles,* calls "the most complete example of Cleopatra's conversion of *slime into fertility*"). At the moment of Cleopatra's death, these ideas re-appear. They do so, because only just behind the stage spectacle of the queen of Egypt in all her glory, is the sense of an outcast from society—gipsy, felon, whatever it may be—baited as the victim of the common people:

> Now, Iras, what think'st thou?
> Thou an Egyptian puppet shall be shown
> In Rome as well as I. Mechanic slaves,
> With greasy aprons, rules, and hammers, shall
> Uplift us to the view; in their thick breaths,
> Rank of gross diet, shall we be enclouded. ...
>   (V.ii.206)

In this, she is merely rehearsing what Antony already described in his moment of rage with her:

> Let him take thee
> And hoist thee up to the shouting Plebeians;
>   ...most monster-like be shown
> For poor'st diminutives, for doits, and let

> Patient Octavia plough thy visage up
> With her prepared nails.   (IV.xii.33)

Though the appearance of Cleopatra in the moment of her death may be great and splendid, the reality comes close to that very different idea of death, drawing upon all these passages, which comes into her mind when she is first captured:

> Know, sir, that I
> Will not wait pinion'd at your master's court,
> Nor once be chastis'd by the sober eye
> Of dull Octavia. Shall they hoist me up,
> And show me to the shouting varletry
> Of censuring Rome? Rather a ditch in Egypt
> Be gentle grave unto me! Rather on Nilus' mud
> Lay me stark-naked, and let the water-flies
> Blow me into abhorring! Rather make
> My country's high Pyramides my gibbet,
> And hang me up in chains!   (V.ii.52)

—outcast or outlaw, it is with images like these that the play surrounds Cleopatra's death in our imaginations. Caesar's closing tribute to the nobleness of both queen and servants fuses with a sense of Cleopatra's having been brought to the level of humanity at its simplest and most primitive; to the bedrock of life. As near to an animal as a human creature can come, the victim is hunted by his own kind until, with whatever justice and whatever nobility, his life is taken. Death is no mere crowning misfortune; it is almost recognized, by protagonist and pursuers alike, as the stylized act which fitly closes a stylized sequence. This sequence is beginning to seem like a recurrent *motif* in the tragedies. It is the ordeal of the great and alienated who are pursued by life until they are sacrificed.

The Ethic of the Imagination:
Love and Art in *Antony and Cleopatra*

by Robert Ornstein

The last scene of *Antony and Cleopatra* would be less difficult if it were more obviously solemn and serious. There is no
lack of grandeur in the dying Cleopatra, but the comic note struck
in her conversation with the Clown persists and mingles with the
ceremonial mystery of her death. She is amused as well as ecstatic;
when she thinks of Octavius, her visionary glances turn into a
comic wink. She jests with Iras and Charmian, and she plays a
children's game with the asps at her breast. It is difficult, of
course, to complain about a scene that comes so very near the
sublime. But now and then we may wish that Cleopatra had a
more sober view of her own catastrophe, which she treats as a
marriage feast (not where she eats, but where she is eaten), a
tender domestic scene, an apotheosis, and a practical joke on the
universal landlord.

Those who see no majesty in the earlier Cleopatra argue that
the glitter of the Monument scene is not gold or complain that
the Cleopatra of the last act is a new and exalted creature fashioned
for the sake of a resplendent artistic conclusion. But for most of us
the problem of the last scene is not focused in Cleopatra's character
as such. Here at least her emotions are translucent: she has no
thought but of Antony and no desire except to join him in death.
What vexes us is Cleopatra's immortal longings. For even as we
cannot resist the spell of her rapturous lyricism, neither can we

"The Ethic of the Imagination: Love and Art in *Antony and Cleopatra*," by
Robert Ornstein. From *Later Shakespeare, Stratford-upon-Avon Studies 8:*
edited by John Russell Brown and Bernard Harris (London: Edward Arnold
Ltd., 1966), pp. 31-46. Copyright © 1966 by Edward Arnold (Publishers) Ltd.
Reprinted by kind permission of Edward Arnold (Publishers) Ltd., London, and
the author.

assent to her vision of eternal love, which is embarrassingly physical, and worse still, smacks of a literary conventionality—of the Petrarchan "forever." We expect Cleopatra to dream of a long love's day since she is a creature of illusion. But we are not ready to equate her dream with Shakespeare's vision of love, which, in the sonnets at least, belongs very much to this world. Unlike other Renaissance poets, Shakespeare does not deny the brief hours and weeks of human love; it is enough for him that love triumphs *to* the edge of doom.

There would be no problem in the final scene if there were an Enobarbus to comment on Cleopatra's immortal longings as he comments on Antony's attempts to outstare the lightning; or if there were a Charmian, immune to her mistress's self-intoxication, to mock Cleopatra's last imaginings. Octavius disappoints us by speaking ambiguously of Cleopatra's "strong toil of grace"; and before him there is only the Clown, who speaks paradoxically of "a very honest woman, but something given to the lie, as a woman should not do, but in the way of honesty." Are we to assume that Cleopatra is at her death a very honest woman but something given to the lie? The question of honesty is very important in the play: Enobarbus and his honesty begin to square; Antony's misfortunes corrupt honest men; and Octavius' words to Cleopatra bear little relation to his thoughts. We have heard Cleopatra lie many times before, even as we have seen Antony again and again turn his back on reality. An honest thought would almost seem out of place among the illusions, charms, and enchantments of Egypt. It is a land of dreaming, playing, and acting, where deaths are not quite deaths (or not quite believable); where illnesses, like tears, are profuse but only momentary; and where spectacles like that at Cydnus and the Monument are contrived to seduce the senses and the imagination. We have to admit that Cleopatra's barge, which Enobarbus describes as the purest mythic fancy, is a glorious and very honest illusion. But her death scene, which is a second Cydnus, is more difficult to judge because it envisions a reality that is past the size of dreaming and it seems to demand from us an impossible act of poetic faith. Shall we say than some jesting about the worm alters the fact of Cleopatra's death, or that her queenly robes make Octavius' victory illusory? She speaks of the babes milking her breast, but the drowsiness she feels is of death, not of maternal fulfilment.

We lose the profounder meanings of *Antony and Cleopatra* if we insist that questions of truth and honesty are irrelevant to Cleopatra or that her splendid poetic vision is beyond reason itself. For nothing less is at stake in the final scene than the honesty of the imagination and the superiority of its truths to the facts of imperial conquest. What we share with Cleopatra is not a visionary experience but the delight of her conspiracy with the Clown that unpolicies Octavius. She is used to playing jokes on these Romans, and her skill as a comedian shines brightly in the farce of the Seleucus episode, and in the irony of her grave submission to the sole sir of the world. Even as she earlier tormented Antony with references to the immortal Fulvia ("Can Fulvia die?"), in the last Act her thoughts dwell humorously on Octavia, the Roman matron, who is demurely sharpening her fingernails in anticipation of Cleopatra's arrival in Rome. There is so much laughter earlier in the play that the comedy of the last Act does not surprise us. It does bother us, however, because we think that the story of Antony and Cleopatra should have been as tragic to Shakespeare as it was to the illustrators of De Casibus tales and to Shakespeare's French and English contemporaries. Or if we do not insist that it is tragic despite its final mood of joyous triumph and release, then we would have it an ironic comedy like *Troilus and Cressida,* in which ageing sensual love is shadowed by deceptions, jealousies, and fears. Ignoring the contrary evidence of the poetry, we imagine a relatively detached Shakespeare, who could delight in the paradoxical qualities of his lovers, but who would not have us take their professions at face value.

Most of the ironies in *Antony and Cleopatra* are not present in Plutarch's account, because they arise from the extravagant declarations and sublime aspirations which Shakespeare gives to his lovers. Antony would die a bridegroom, but his longing is prompted by the lie of Cleopatra's death, and he fails to imitate the noble Roman suicide of Eros. Cleopatra melts into lyric grief but she will not open the Monument, and so Antony must be hauled aloft to die in her arms. Then he speaks bravely of dying in the high Roman fashion but equivocates with life, charms Dolabella, and trifles with Seleucus before she shackles up all accidents. Even as we list these ironic episodes, however, we wonder if irony is the primary effect which these scenes have upon an audience. And when we take a larger view of plot we see that again and again irony is transformed into paradox by a felicitous turn of events that offers to the lovers something like the second chance given to the characters of the late romances. Though only for a dying moment, Antony and Cleopatra have the opportunity to call back yesterday, and to rediscover the love which they had thought was lost forever. Indeed, if Antony's death in Cleopatra's arms is a mocking irony, then it is an irony devoutly to be wished for.

Though some critics dwell on Antony's disillusionment, his rages more often approach the melodramatic hyperbole of Leontes' speeches than the torments of Troilus'; in fact Antony is most comic when he takes a high moral tone with his Egyptian dish and laments his Roman pillow left unpressed. We are urbane enough, of course, to admit some joking about adultery in *The Winter's Tale*. We smile at the thought of Sir Smiles fishing in his neighbour's pond because we know that Hermione is chaste. But we would have a more serious view of sexuality in *Antony and Cleopatra* because Cleopatra's innocence is only a pose and her fidelity is open to question. Why should her promiscuous past be cheerfully dismissed as "salad days"? And why should the lack of honesty in women, which is so bitter a theme in *Hamlet* and *Troilus and Cressida*, be reduced at last to the Clown's silly joke? If we assume that a personal disillusion lies behind the view of sex in the great tragedies, then we can infer from *Antony and Cleopatra* (as from the late romances) that in time Shakespeare recovered from the sexual nausea and sickness of generation expressed in *Hamlet* and *King Lear*. But biographical interpretations are at best dubious; what we find in *Antony and Cleopatra* is not a changed attitude towards sexual love, but rather a new perspective on the relations between the sexes. In his great tragedies and in the problem comedies, Shakespeare is concerned with the masculine view of sex. Hamlet's lines, for example, express a typically masculine contempt for woman's frailty and a masculine horror at the sexuality that breeds generations of sinners. Similarly Troilus and Othello are haunted by the masculine desire for sexual possession, a desire that is accompanied by the fear of loss and of the general mock. The darker side of romantic (i.e. masculine) ideals of fidelity is revealed in the anguish of the corrupted Moor, who would not keep a corner in the thing he loved for others' uses.

Where the masculine hunger is for sexual possession and domination, Cleopatra's womanly desire is to be possessed, and to

triumph in surrendering. She would be taken; she would yield
and feel again the weight of Antony. In his moments of rage,
Antony is tormented by the thought that other men have enjoyed
Cleopatra. Her womanly jealousies are of another kind: she
envies in Fulvia and Octavia the title and place of a "married
woman." Only superficially does the imagery of feeding in *Antony
and Cleopatra* recall that of *Troilus and Cressida,* for Cleopatra's
lines do not express the pang of unsatisfied appetite or of frustrate
longing; her thoughts linger over the delicious memory of a fulfilment that is maternal as well as sexual. She has borne the weight
of Antony in her womb as on her body; she has fed the lover and the
babes at her breast. It is striking, moreover, how often Cleopatra's
sexuality is an emotion recollected, not an immediate desire. Her
scenes with Antony are filled with talk of war, with wranglings, and
reconciliations. Only when Antony is absent is Cleopatra's thought
"erotic," and then her longing is not of the flesh but of the total
being, one that is rapturously satisfied by news of Antony. In an
ageing Falstaff passion is merely ludicrous; but the love which
survives the wrinkles and grey hairs that Shakespeare adds to
Plutarch's portrait of the lovers is not quite Time's fool. The
injurious gods cannot cheat Cleopatra as the stars cheat Juliet,
because she has known years of love and revelry with Antony.
Even the sorrow she feels in bearing his dying weight is transmuted by the memory of their earlier dyings. And if her last
dream of Antony is an illusion, it is an illusion born out of the
deepest reality of her experience—she is again for Cydnus.

Vaster than orgiastic memory, the past touches every character
and every scene of *Antony and Cleopatra.* We hear of Antony's
former greatness as a soldier, of Caesar and Pompey, Brutus and
Cassius. The historical events depicted in *Julius Caesar* are recalled, and the past seems to live again in the present as Antony
takes Brutus' place as Octavius' antagonist, and as once again love
is opposed to imperial ambition. The ruthless impersonalism of
the Triumvirate depicted in *Julius Caesar* lives on in the cold
efficiency of Octavius, and the fidelity which the defeated Brutus
inspired is reflected again in the deaths of Antony and Cleopatra
and of those who loved them. To look back at *Julius Caesar* is to
realize that Shakespeare did not expediently darken his portrayal of Rome in *Antony and Cleopatra* in order to soften our
judgement of Egypt. He saw Caesar's ambition as a symptom of
the decay of the Roman state, and he saw the decline of Roman

political idealism as a process which had begun even before the assassination of Caesar unloosed the spirit of empire in Antony and Octavius. The end of an era of nobility was marked in *Julius Caesar* by the execution of a hundred Senators and by the suicides of Portia, Cassius, Titinius, and Brutus. In *Antony and Cleopatra* the decay of Roman idealism is so advanced that it is difficult to say whether a Roman thought is of duty or of disloyalty. Yet the decay of the Roman state is paradoxical, because it is not a melting into Egyptian softness but a hardening into the marble-like ruthlessness of the universal landlord. No trace of Brutus' stoicism remains in Octavius' Rome; the prevailing philosophy is the cynical prudence of the Fool's songs in *Lear*. Weakness is merely despised, misfortune corrupts honest soldiers, and loyalty belongs only to the rising man. The pattern of Roman history unfolds for us on Pompey's galley. At present Rome is led by men who (with the exception of Octavius) would rather feast than rule and who make treaties of convenience they do not intend to keep. The Rome that was is recalled by Pompey, who is kept from treachery, not by a personal sense of honour, but by a memory of the honour once sacred to Rome—by a nostalgia for the ethic of his father. Unable to play falsely, Pompey loses the future, which belongs to a Menas who will desert the half-corrupted Pompey, and to an Octavius, whose honour demands only the justification of unscrupulousness. Far more than in the days of Brutus, Rome is bent on empire and rules by the sword; yet compared to the past, the present is not a time of great soldiery. The continual talk of war only emphasizes that the great military exploits live in memory. All the leaders, including Antony, deal in lieutenantry, and their lieutenants fear to win great victories. Except for the moment when Antony and Scarus beat back Octavius' legions, the battlefield is not a place where honour is won. It is a place where great men defeat themselves; it is the scene of shameful weakness or of the shameless policy that places revolted legions in the van.

The echoes of a nobler past are important because they remind us that the Rome which Octavius rules is not the eternal reality of political life. Only here and now must men like Enobarbus choose between the ways of soldiery and of personal loyalty, that were before a single path. But even as Shakespeare bounds his present scene by placing it in a larger historical framework, his use of archetypal imagery suggests that the worlds of Rome and

Egypt are eternal aspects of human experience and form a dichotomy as elemental as that of male and female. The hard masculine world of Rome is imaged in sword, armour, and terms of war, in geometry and stone, and in the engineering that builds or destroys. The soft yielding feminine world of Egypt is poetically imaged as uniting the artifices of sexual temptation to the naturalness of fecundity and to the processes of growth and decay which depend on sun, wind, and water. But the absolute distinctions between Rome and Egypt which the imagery enforces are qualified by the dramatic action, that reveals the extent to which these worlds are mirror images of one another and divergent expressions of the same fundamental human impulses. Although by Roman standards, Antony is unmanned, the Roman standard of masculinity is itself examined by the dramatic action and found deficient. Moreover, although Antony's decline in Egypt is from the Roman measure, his decline also measures the decay of the Roman ideal of soldiery.

The tension between image and plot in *Antony and Cleopatra* leads again and again to paradox. The patterns of imagery insist that Egypt is a Circean land of mandragora and lotus-eaters, where sensuality breeds forgetfulness of Rome and duty. But the action shows us that it is Cleopatra, the Serpent of Old Nile, not Antony, who would hear the Roman messengers; and it is Cleopatra, not Octavia, who demands her place in the war by Antony's side. Thus it may not be completely ironic that the finest Roman words of the play are spoken by Cleopatra to Antony in Act I, Scene iii:

> Your honour calls you hence,
> Therefore be deaf to my unpitied folly,
> And all the gods go with you! Upon your sword
> Sit laurel victory, and smooth success
> Be strew'd before your feet!

The imagery contrasts the enduring monumental quality of Rome to the melting evanescence of Egypt. But the Roman leaders know that the marble-constancy of Rome is founded precariously on the shifting loyalties of a disaffected populace and is forever subject to the battering ram of ambition. The violent spasms of destruction common to Rome are alien to Egypt, where there is permanence in the recurring cycle of growth and decay that dungs the earth, and where the bounty of the Nile requires that nothing be cultivated except the human sensibility. While the imagery insists upon the oversophisticated appetites of Egypt, the Roman leaders tell of wars that make men drink the stale of horses and eat flesh that men die to look upon. Recurrent allusions to snare, serpent, toil, and charm depict Cleopatra as archetypal temptress and seducer. And yet there is no Egyptian snare or temptation as degrading as that which Menas offers Pompey or that which Octavius twice offers Cleopatra. How, indeed, shall we compare Cleopatra's toils with the politic duplicities of Octavius, who tries to patch a quarrel with Antony, engineers the cynical proposal of the marriage to Octavia, and breaks his treaty with Pompey and his bond with Lepidus? The lies of Egypt are amateurish compared with those of Octavius and of the trustworthy Proculeius; not one Roman speaks the truth to Cleopatra at the end except Dolabella, and he must be seduced into telling the truth.

I do not mean that we are supposed to shudder at Rome. Though its political principles have decayed, it is in other respects a healthy and capable world, led by an Octavius who is cold not inhuman, unprincipled yet eminently respectable. His ambition is not seen as an anarchic force in an ordered world, it is rather the normal bent of a society shaped by masculine ideals of politics and power. Morally there is not much to choose between Rome and Egypt; in matters of the heart and of the imagination, however, they are polar opposites. Where Antony and Cleopatra's thoughts have a cosmic poetic amplitude, the Roman measure of bigness is earthbound and philistine; its imagination stirs at thoughts of triumphal spectacle und arch. (Octavius would have the trees bear men and the dust ascend to heaven when his sister enters Rome.) Untouched by art, and unsoftened by feminine influence, the Romans pride themselves on their masculine hardness and reticence. Cold, and to temptation slow, they scorn tears and womanish emotion. Despite the protective attitude they adopt, they are crass and patronizing in their relations with women whom they value as sexual objects and political pawns. Cleopatra rightly fears Antony's callousness because she knows that by Roman standards she is a diversion that should not be missed or overprized. The coarseness of the Roman view of sex is apparent throughout the play—in the lines of Octavius as well as Enobarbus, in Pompey's smutty jests, and in the salacious eagerness of Caesar's lieutenants to hear tales of Cleopatra. Although

Enobarbus describes her lightness, her artfulness, her wit, and her infinite variety, the other Romans (like so many modern critics) can picture her only in the conventional posture of a whore, drugging Antony with cloying lascivious wassails.

In most respects the priggish Octavius is the very opposite of Antony. In his treatment of women, however, he is Antony's Roman brother. Antony adopts the pose of Cleopatra's general when he flees his Egyptian "dotage." Octavius sends Thyreus to Cleopatra with solemn assurances that her honour is unsullied. Antony babbles to Octavia about his honour when he deserts her; Octavius marries his sister to a man he despises and then wars to erase her dishonour. Octavius, like Antony, hungers for Cleopatra but his desire to possess her is more shameless and more contemptible. Indifferent to Antony's fate (he would be content if Cleopatra murders her lover), he lies to Cleopatra, cajoles her, and threatens her children in order to keep her alive so that she may be displayed as his trophy in Rome. He has no doubt that a woman like Cleopatra will be seduced into ignobleness when

> want will perjure
> The ne'er-touched vestal.

Warm and generous as well as callous, Antony is able to respond to the arts of Egypt, and he is so deeply altered by his response that it is difficult to say what is Antony or when he is less than Antony or when he is himself again. A legend in his lifetime, he is the hero of fantastic exploits and the stuff of soldierly brags and mythic imaginings. Contemning his Egyptian dotage, Philo, Demetrius, and Octavius recall a plated Mars and contrast Antony's earlier feats of battle to his present wassails. But Cleopatra and Enobarbus remember another, more sensual, Antony—Plutarch's gamester and reveller, the lover of plays in *Julius Caesar,* who did not learn the arts of dissipation in Egypt or desert them when he returns to Rome. When plagued by his Roman conscience, Antony sees his salvation in a flight from Egypt; in Rome he momentarily recovers his ability to command, which allows him to look over Octavius' head. But Antony is not reinspired by Roman ideals; on the contrary, his superiority is a personal honesty that contrasts with Octavius' devious and politic attempts to provoke a quarrel. No salvation awaits Antony in Rome because there is no honourable purpose to engage him; the Triumvirate feasts and gambles and despises the populace. The only Roman dedication is Octavius' desire to be the sole sir of the world. Moreover, if Antony's faults are Egyptian, he does not lose them in Rome, where he displays the very weaknesses that are later to destroy him: a desire to put off issues and to escape unpleasantness. In Egypt he is led by Cleopatra; in Rome he is led by Octavius' lieutenants into the foolish expediency of the marriage to Octavia. There is no point in the play, therefore, at which we can say, here Antony falls. His decline is a process that began in years past and which seems the inevitable destiny of a sensualist and opportunist who never shared Octavius' ambition to possess the entire world, but who wanted empires to play with and superfluous kings to feast and do his bidding. If we must have a reason for Antony's decline, we can say that he lost the desire before he lost the ability to command. He is never defeated in battle during the play. After the disaster at Actium, his fleet is intact and his army powerful though kings and legions desert. A doting braggart might have brushed aside the reality of his cowardice at sea; but Antony is shattered by the very trait which ennobled him in his dealings with Octavius, by an honourable shame at his failings as a leader.

It is characteristic of the handling of events in *Antony and Cleopatra* that we do not see Antony's failure of nerve at Actium; we see Canidius', Scarus', and Enobarbus' response to it, and, following that, we see Antony's reaction. Much use is made of messengers bearing tidings of conflict, disaster, and death, because this is a play of reaction rather than of action. We know Octavius, Cleopatra, Enobarbus, Pompey, and Lepidus by the way that they respond to news of Antony. And we know Antony by his response to Cleopatra and to his fading powers, by his alternating moods of depression and elation, by his moments of impotent rage or of bluster, when he will outstare the lightning, and by his reconciliations with Cleopatra. This vacillation of mood in Antony reminds us of Richard II, except that Richard's journey is towards the nihilism of endlessly circling thoughts, while Antony becomes a fuller man in his decline, more bounteous in his love and in his generosity. When he tries to express, after the second disaster at sea, his loss of soldierly identity, he convinces us that he has changed, not lost, his identity. The soldier has become a lover, the spendthrift a mine of bounty, and the callous opportunist a meditative poet.

The growth of poetic sensitivity in Antony was apparent to earlier generations of critics. It is less apparent to us, ironically,

because our desire to read Shakespeare "poetically" blurs our
awareness of the poetic attributes of the characters in the plays.
And to avoid critical naïvete, we make artificial distinctions
between the form and substance of Shakespeare's dramatic verse.
When Antony compares his state to the evanescent shapelessness
of clouds in a dying afternoon, we grant to him the sense of
weariness and loss which the lines convey; but the heavenly
imagery and the poetic sensibility revealed in this passage we
reserve for Shakespeare, who, we say, merely lends Antony his
poetic faculty for artistic purposes. But it is only a step from this
"sophisticated" approach to Antony's speeches to the notion that
the morbidity of Hamlet's soliloquies is "saved" by the nobility
of Shakespeare's poetry. If we grant Hamlet the nobility of his
utterances, how shall we deny Antony his poetry? Not all the
characters who speak in verse are poetic. Although Octavius'
lines are at times richly metaphorical, he seems to us thoroughly
prosaic, because the impression of poetic sensibility in Shakespeare's characters depends upon the nature of their response to
life, not on the mere presence of figurative language in their
speeches. Who but a poet would see the clouds as Antony does,
and who but a poet would remember this heavenly image at the
point of death? Antony's leave-taking of the world is an imaginative reverie untouched by the grandiosity that marks so many of
his early "poetic" declarations.

At the beginning of the play it is obvious that Antony does not
know Cleopatra because he does not yet know what is evident to
the audience, that his only desire is to be with this woman. We
feel that the hyperbole of his early speeches is strained, because
his extravagant professions of love are undercut by his harsh,
grating response to news from Rome and by his sensitivity to the
Roman view of Cleopatra. Though he says here is my space, he
is unable to conceive of a world limited by love; and he is un-
aware that he uses Cleopatra to excuse his indifference to political
issues. We smile at Cleopatra's role of betrayed innocence, but not
at her keen perception of the emotional dishonesty of Antony's
gestures of devotion and of the callousness that underlies them.
She knows how easily an Antony who shrugs off Fulvia's death
may desert her in turn. The first scenes show us an Antony who is
caught between what he tells Cleopatra, and in part believes, and
what he tells himself about her, and in part believes. In Rome he

is irritated by every reference to her; he never speaks her name though his is always on her lips, and he never regards her as an equal or as having any claims upon him. When he decides to return to Egypt, he speaks of her as his pleasure.

As Antony's world shrinks, his hyperbole becomes, paradoxically, more convincing. When he is confronted by Octavius' legions, his chivalric pose becomes more than a pose, because at last he does fight for Cleopatra; and thus his arming before battle with Cleopatra's aid is more than one last parody of medieval romance. Now when Antony acts, he is aware of his pretendings; tutored by Cleopatra, he imitates after Actium her celerity in dying and, like her, he plays on the feelings of those who love him, making Enobarbus onion-eyed. His talk of death and his shaking of hands is an artful appeal to his followers' emotion and yet an honest piece of acting, because it expresses a true warmth and generosity of spirit. There are times, of course, when Antony's gestures are less honest, when he abuses Cleopatra for her treachery. But his Herculean rages are short lived and his self-pity is untouched by genuine suffering. His despondency is always more painful to those who love him than it is to Antony, who is never deeply in conflict with himself, and who is more a spectator to, than a participant in, the final disaster at sea. His catastrophes are strangely beautiful: his gods desert to music, his loss of empire is signalled by shouts of joy in the fleets. Even at his nadir he shakes hands with Fortune as with an old familiar friend.

Whatever ironies attach to the manner of Antony's death, he is raised visually, and poetically, above the earth on which the melancholy Enobarbus sinks. The moralizing critic interprets Antony's fate as a warning to adhere to the path of reason; he forgets that Enobarbus follows reason to a fate more wretched than Antony's. Enobarbus chooses Rome lest he lose himself in Antony's dotage and like Antony be made a woman. In itself this choice is not shameful; Enobarbus' act has a hundred Roman precedents, and he has no reason—or, at least, no Roman reason —to follow a leader who can no longer command. What is shameful is Enobarbus' betrayal of himself, because he allows his reason and his honesty to square. Worse still, he goes over to Octavius knowing that to have stayed with Antony was to have "won a place in the story." Yet the place which Enobarbus wins is not as ignoble as he thinks, for we sense that his desertion of Antony is, like his death, an act of love. He leaves Antony when he can no longer bear to watch Antony's failure as a general, and he is redeemed by his response to Antony's generosity even though he has no chance to express to his master the full measure of his devotion. The lie of Cleopatra's death saves Antony from Enobarbus' fate because it ends the lie of his rage while Cleopatra is still alive. And Antony's failure to die in the high Roman fashion makes possible the final expression of his bounteous love, his dying wish that she save herself by making terms with Octavius.

Between the disaster at Actium and his final reunion with Cleopatra, Antony is the centre of the dramatic action. At the Monument, however, the dramatic focus shifts: the dying Antony plays the chorus to Cleopatra's impassioned grief, and she is from that moment on the supreme figure of the play. At Antony's death, we are told, a new Cleopatra is born—the wanton temptress rises to regal majesty. But what is really new in the Cleopatra who mourns over Antony? Her royalty, her poetic sensibility, and her capacity for profound emotion were evident before; her grief is hardly surprising when, from the beginning, her every thought is of Antony, and she is haunted by the fear of losing him. Is it the new Cleopatra who says, "Husband, I come? Or is she the same Egyptian who in the first scene of the play reveals her envy of Fulvia, the *married woman,* and her longing to be more to Antony than his pleasure?

Only Shakespeare could have imagined that the greatest courtesan of all time hungered to be Antony's wife—to be made "an honest woman." Only he could have dreamed of a Cleopatra who is, despite her lies and pretendings, always emotionally honest. When the messenger brings news of Antony's remarriage, she is furious, but her fury is directed at the messenger, not at Antony. If she pretends to die when Antony leaves her, it is because their partings are a form of death which leaves only the desire to sleep and dream of Antony. Those who read her thoughts announce that she intends to betray him when she listens to Thyreus. The text indicates only the elaborate irony of her submission and her comic surprise at Octavius' concern for her honour. It is quite explicit, moreover, that Enobarbus is able to uncover Cleopatra's intended treachery only because she insists that he be present at the interview with Thyreus. How foolish of this cunning woman to plan a betrayal of Antony in the presence of Enobarbus! What we witness is not Cleopatra's duplicity but Enobarbus' jealous revenge and the confusion of rage in Antony, who has Thyreus whipped for kiss-ing the "kingly" hand of that "boggler" Cleopatra.

According to Plutarch, Cleopatra demanded a role in the war against Octavius because she feared that in her absence Antony and Octavius might be reconciled. Shakespeare fails to give Cleopatra a similar explicit motive. Against Enobarbus' warning and against her own nature, she insists upon bearing a charge in the war; she will have Antony fight by sea so that she may command her fleet at Actium. If Cleopatra were nothing more than the seductress whom critics describe, her desire to fight by Antony's side would seem to us incredible. It does not astonish us, however, because we see from the beginning her desire to be worthy of this Herculean Roman, and to imitate the noble Roman fashion of words and deeds. She bids a Roman farewell to Antony in the first Act even as she seeks a Roman death in the last art. Her desire to be a Roman wife, which becomes explicit at her death, leads Cleopatra to attempt at Actium the role of Fulvia, the only part she plays falsely before Antony.

Like Antony, Cleopatra does not die in the high Roman fash-ion; and though she earns the title of Antony's wife she remains more Egyptian than Roman, more various than marble-constant. Timidity, vanity, and womanly fears plague her Roman resolu-tion; she dies a sensual creature of the Nile, artful, theatrical, jealous to the end of Antony. Part of the mystery of her death is the fullness with which it expresses the multiplicity of her nature. She is Antony's mistress and his wife, the graceful courtesan and the tender mother, the great queen and the simple lass. Her drowsiness is at once sensual, maternal, and child-like, for though she nurses her imaginary babes, she is, as so many times before, very like a child, who plays now at being mother, and who is dressed in a royal costume to surprise Octavius. Her crown slips, but Charmian mends it before she too plays.

More than a triumph over Octavius, Cleopatra's death is a triumph over her own fears and over a deeply rooted instinct for life. She is not, however, in love with death though she allows it to commit a loving act upon her; she dreams of life and of Antony. And though she makes a fellow-conspirator of the worm which will eat her, she knows it is not worth the feeding; she knows too the horror of physical decay, which she has envisioned before in striking images of fly-blown bodies. Her death will not be a melting into eternal natural change; it will be a change

into changelessness that robs Octavius of his victory and that
mocks his immortal longings. He thinks that Cleopatra's "life in
Rome/ Would be eternal in our triumph" and he meditates in
his last speech on the glory he has won by the deaths of the lovers.
But it is paltry to be Caesar, whose quest of fame earns an ig-
nominious place in the story.

Cleopatra's sense of the comedy of imperial ambition is not a
new intuition that reaches "beyond the tragic." The paltriness of
Caesar was evident to the youthful Shakespeare, whose sonnets
contrast the vital power of art to the lifeless marble and gilded
monuments of princes. There are echoes of the sonnets, I think,
in the antithesis of Egypt and Rome, and in the depiction of a
love which finally admits not even the impediment of death. The
themes of the sonnets are also relevant to the echoes in the final
scene of Capulet's Monument, where another pair of lovers found
in death the marriage union which life denied. As *Romeo and
Juliet* draws to a close, we sense that the true memorial to the
lovers is not the gilded statues which Montague and Capulet
promise to raise, but Shakespeare's play. And we know that
Cleopatra will live in art because she fashions her own incomparable memorial, the scene in the Monument, which overshadows
the mythic wonder of Cydnus. It is the artist in Cleopatra who
stirs Shakespeare's deepest imaginative sympathies and who receives the immeasurable bounty of his artistic love, which is
immortality itself.

We need not turn *Antony and Cleopatra* into an allegory of
art to see that its final paradox is the final paradox of Donne's
"Canonization": though deserted by those who observe Octavius'
face, the lovers die and rise the same, and prove mysterious by
their love. The defect of their passion becomes perfection because ultimately theirs is not a sublunary love: their "faults"
shine like the unchanging stars. Donne's lover is a poet who
builds in sonnets' pretty rooms, and who fashions the legend of
his love in immortal verse. Cleopatra is an artist who fashions
out of her life a legend that is unfit for hearse or for Octavius'
half-acre tombs. Her "place in the story" is beside the legendary
figures who live in ancient myth. She is another Thetis, an Isis,
a Venus, a Dido; Cupids and Nereides attend her, the winds are
enamoured of her, and she is wooed by Phoebus and, at last, by
Death himself. She teaches a plated Mars an artful way of loving;
and she turns this demi-Atlas after death into a very god who

spreads the masculine seed of his inexhaustible bounty over the earth. In her mythopeic imagination Antony bestrides the ocean, making cities on the waves, and creating empires through a divinely prodigal carelessness—he drops realms and islands out of his pockets.

The foolish Clown is right after all. The biting of Cleopatra's worms is immortal, because it brings a death that lives in the artistic imagination. She dies in the last scene of Shakespeare's play as she has died so many times before in Plutarch, in medieval "tragedy," and in Renaissance plays and poems. And because Shakespeare has written, she will die many times again and be staged over and over to the show—so long as men can breathe or eyes can see, Cleopatra is again for Cydnus. The terms *act, play,* and *show* are not metaphorical when applied to her, because she is in her essential being an actress. Her poses are too extravagant to deceive; they are meant to bewitch and captivate by their infinite variety. She will not allow herself to be carted through the streets of Rome in the posture of a whore or to be staged to the show in vulgar Roman fashion. But as if she knows that her destiny is art, she dons her robes and prepares one last dazzling scene that draws a gasp of admiration from Octavius. We have seen her metamorphoses before—her sudden changes from tears to laughter, from pettiness to regality, and from sickness to health. None of them is comparable, however, to the metamorphosis of her death, which turns life into art.

As early as the sonnets, Shakespeare knew that the enemy of love is not time or death; these can only refine its worth. Love's adversary is the unfeeling heart—those who are "as stone/ Unmoved, cold and to temptation slow." He can accept a world of mutability in *Antony and Cleopatra,* as in the tragedies and the late romances, because it offers the possibility of renewing change, in later generations, and in the heart of a Lear, an Antony, or a Leontes. Shakespeare does not retreat in his later plays from the exalted humanism of his tragedies, which stresses the irreplaceableness of a Cordelia; he does not find comfort in a naturalistic faith in the continuance of life. The security of *Antony and Cleopatra* and of the late romances is founded on the paradox of tragic art, which depicts immeasurable loss and yet preserves forever that which the artist supremely values. Although great creating Nature may reincarnate some of the rareness of Hermione in Perdita, the true miracle of *The Winter's Tale* is Paulina's art, which preserves and enriches the wonder of Hermione herself.

In Shakespeare's great tragedies illusion and seeming are opposed to moral reality. But in Cleopatra's artful spectacles as in the masques of Prospero and Paulina, illusion and reality intermingle. Sober realists may agree with Dolabella that the Antony whom Cleopatra ecstatically recalls is only a dream of her imagination; they forget, however, that Dolabella, like Cleopatra, is only a dream of Shakespeare's imagination. The triumph of love and art in *Antony and Cleopatra* will not allow us to believe that Shakespeare, who celebrated in the sonnets the miracle of poetry, expressed in Prospero's lines a disillusioned awareness of the vanity of his dramatic art. After a lifetime spent in creating the magic of the stage, Shakespeare must have known that the "idle" dreamlike play of an artist's imagination is the deepest reality of his experience, if not a clue to the fundamental reality of all experience:

> We are such stuff
> As dreams are made on, and our little life
> Is rounded with a sleep.

Past the Size of Dreaming

by Bernard Beckerman

What are the dimensions of *Antony and Cleopatra?* Is it truly "a vast canvas" depicting the clash of empires? Is it indeed "the most spacious" of Shakespeare's plays? Its epic stature is so generally conceded that only an eccentric would suggest that, far from being monumental, *Antony and Cleopatra* is delicate as porcelain, fragile as a lyric of elusive affection.[1] Yet so odd and mysterious has the play's history been, both in the library and on the stage, that even such eccentricity may be justified in order to examine its idiosyncratic nature anew.

At first glance *Antony and Cleopatra* seems to be a sprawling spectacle. Theatrically and imaginatively it overflows the customary bounds of the drama. Its forty two scenes are the greatest number that Shakespeare ever crammed into one play. Leaping from Egypt to Rome and back to Egypt, they create an image of world-ranging events. The names, Antony, Cleopatra, and Caesar ring out like a roster of the gods. An imperial atmosphere permeates the stage. And yet, these impressions belie the heart of the action. Though the play shows the fall of an empire, little time is devoted to how political and military events turn out. There is one scene of negotiation between Antony and Caesar, but that quickly focuses upon a marital issue. And crucial though battles

"Past the Size of Dreaming," by Bernard Beckerman. Published here by permission of Bernard Beckerman, Professor of Dramatic Arts, Columbia University. This essay appears in print for the first time in this volume. Quotations from *Antony and Cleopatra* follow the text edited by M.R. Ridley as published in the Arden edition (1954).

[1]A. C. Bradley uses the phrase "vast canvas" in his Oxford lecture on *Antony and Cleopatra* (1905) and Harley Granville-Barker begins his preface to the drama with the assertion: "Here is the most spacious of [Shakespeare's] plays" (1930). Maynard Mack, on the other hand, does point out the "delicacy" of the play in his perceptive essay, *"Antony and Cleopatra:* The Stillness and the Dance," printed in *Shakespeare's Art,* ed. M. Crane (Chicago: 1973), p. 80.

are to the fortunes of Antony, Shakespeare does not dwell on the fighting itself. Instead, our attention is repeatedly directed to the subtle motions of thought and feeling passing between Antony and Cleopatra.

The play falls into two main parts. During the first part the prevailing impulse, to the extent there is one, comes from Antony. He endeavors to accommodate the demands of his political and military position to his desire for things Egyptian. The hinge of the narrative, at almost the exact center of the play, occurs early in the third act when he finally abandons Rome and gives himself to Egypt unreservedly. The second part of the narrative traces his attempt to accommodate his allegiance to Cleopatra with the need to defend himself politically and militarily.

For Shakespeare such bifurcated story-telling is not uncommon. What is uncommon is the way he has joined the two parts of *Antony and Cleopatra.* In all the major tragedies preceding this one, Shakespeare raised the final moments of part one to a high pitch. Invariably the third act unfolds in a series of explosions which are the hero's reactions to the dramatic imperatives facing him. Hamlet moves from the exultance of unmasking Claudius in the play-within-the-play scene to the painful restraint of not slaying the orant Claudius and finally to the frenzied harangue with which he assaults his mother. Macbeth is unmanned by the appearances of Banquo's ghost, an experience that cuts him loose, once and for all, from humane constraints. And in the play that best exemplifies the design in Shakespeare's art, *King Lear,* the middle of the play rises to a plateau of maddened passion in which the old king futilely endeavors to reconcile a world of order and degree with the unnatural rejection he has suffered at his daughters' hands. But in *Antony and Cleopatra* there is nothing of this high central plateau of passion. And its absence is all the more curious because in this play Shakespeare is dealing with the overwhelming power of love, a love so hot that neither the fans of reason nor the harsh necessities of fortune can cool it. Yet here, after mastering the art of binding the two-part structure of Elizabethan narrative drama with a knot of sustained trial and passion, he discards the form. And what does he supply in its stead? An approximation of a heightened scene does take the form of a bacchanalia on Pompey's galley (II.vii), but the end of part one comes a little later. Beginning with Act III, scene iii, Shakespeare introduces a rapid montage of accusations and reports which hurtle the antagonists against each other. Cleopatra first adjusts to Antony's new marriage, Antony then separates from Octavia, Octavia reaches Caesar, and through the reports of Caesar and Eros we learn the time of open conflict has arrived. But the shift in narrative is accomplished, however, not by a soul-shattering wrench on Antony's part, but by the reverse, by a vacuum of feeling, a mouthing of claims that indicate inevitability of circumstance rather than exercise of will or passion. That center of emptiness cannot be traced to Plutarch. The source offers considerable transitional material, in the story of Octavia's faithful defense of Antony's home, for instance, to have permitted Shakespeare to exploit the contradictory impulses in Antony's mind. Instead, Shakespeare shows Antony acting out a foreordained role, as though stressing that the barrenness at the heart of the narrative is the issue of the play.

The very first scene of *Antony and Cleopatra* is a clue to all the elements that follow. It is perhaps the most intricate and adroit of all openings by Shakespeare. Not only does it contain the motifs that are later developed, but the very way in which the motifs are dramatized establishes the frame of reference for the entire work. The scene is divided into three parts, the first and third parts serving as a frame for the centered action. The scene begins with a commentary by Philo to another Roman soldier, Demetrius. Philo is criticizing Antony for his infatuation with Cleopatra. As the monarchs enter, he repeatedly advises Demetrius, and through him, the audience to "Look where they come:/ Take but good note ... / Behold and see" (10-13). After they (and with them the audience) watch the exchange between Antony and Cleopatra, the third part begins with Demetrius' astonishment at what he has seen. He expresses sorrow that Antony's behavior confirms what the "common liar" says of him in Rome. Through this arrangement of a three-part scene, Shakespeare produces the effect of making the first and last parts serve as a frame for the middle section. Philo's insistence that we observe what is about to happen and Demetrius' reaction to what he has seen thus give perspective to the central action, and moreover define Rome's relation to Egypt.

In critical literature on this play much is made of the contrast between Rome and Egypt. These two cultures are often represented as having equal emphasis, and Antony is regarded as choosing between the luxuries of the East on one hand and the spartan virtues of the West on the other. But the action of the opening scene belies this interpretation. Instead, the first scene indicates that the acting-out of Antony and Cleopatra's love will occur within a Roman frame of reference. We the audience are invited to see events with Roman eyes, eyes that rarely see anything but the imperfections of Egypt. And though we cannot help being influenced by the Roman view, we are still gods in our own right, as all audiences are, and so we can judge the quality of Rome's view of Antony as we share it. Thus, the opening structure encourages a double vision: the Roman vision and ours that includes yet transcends the Roman vision. That these two views ultimately merge is suggested in the last lines of the play when Caesar, by then the sole "sir" of the world, gives judgment on the pair: "She shall be buried by her Antony./ No grave upon the earth shall clip in it/ A pair so famous." Caesar's words sanction the union of the lovers (they ignore Octavia's rights as wife), and thus are the final expression of a Roman scrutiny that opens the play and persists in scene after scene. That scrutiny stimulates a dynamic state in which Egypt is being judged—and envied—by Rome, not one in which Antony must choose between the two.

In contrast to the framing function of the first and third segments of the opening scene, the central section illustrates the event to be judged. This section prefigures what is to come and reflects in its structure the mode of action for the play as a whole. It begins with four simple sentences:

> *Cleo.* If it be love indeed, tell me how much.
> *Ant.* There's beggary in the love that can be reckon'd.
> *Cleo.* I'll set a bourn how far to be beloved.
> *Ant.* Then must thou needs find out new heaven, new earth.
> (14-17)

These four lines give the musical theme, the thread of melody we shall hear varied throughout the play. The subject is the measure or lack of measure in love. Yet the subject is only the raw material. More important is the motion. We must see through the static emblem of unbounded devotion which these lines seem to promise and discern the conflict they contain. Cleopatra initiates the action by challenging Antony, not only demanding to know the extent of his love, but insinuating in the word "indeed" that what he claims to feel may not "indeed" be love. Antony replies extravagantly if somewhat conventionally, rendering a pat answer to an impossible request. Immediately and yet delicately the actress must convey Cleopatra's mercurial temperament, for her line, "I'll set a bourn how far to be beloved," reverses the challenge. Instead of applauding his dismissal of limited love, she will set bounds to his extravagance. He persists, and expands the dimensions of his affection by directing her to find a new universe to contain it.

This verbal duel is interrupted by a messenger who brings the concerns of Rome into their lives. The intrusion provokes Cleopatra's baiting of Antony and finally Antony's refusal to hear anything of Rome. Two features of this sequence are noteworthy: one, the structure of Cleopatra and Antony's duel, and two, the kind of activity introduced.

First, the structure of the duel. We saw in the first four lines how Cleopatra took the initiative, testing Antony's love. After the messenger is announced, she continues to exercise the initiative, urging Antony to hear the news from Rome, being all the more cutting as he refuses to do so. Gradually, however, as they wrangle, he moves from the defensive to the offensive. Against her mock insistence that he listen to the messengers, Antony exerts a counterforce, his image of their love which he calls "the nobleness of life." He pictures the fulfillment of that love as a form of sport, "Tonight," he says to her, "we'll wander through the streets and note/ The qualities of people" (53-54). Whether such restless sport is a satisfactory realization of their love remains to be seen. What is evident in this middle section, however, is that Antony, provoked by Cleopatra it is true, takes the initiative and sweeping aside all other concerns gives himself completely to the perfecting of their love.

This simple structure then, in which Cleopatra's teasing and testing yield to Antony's overriding image of rapture, serves as a paradigm—a schematic outline, as it were—for all the action of the play. In Shakespeare's hands, it is a particularly potent paradigm, for it is full of fruitful contradictions. Contradiction one: Idealized love can and cannot exclude the demands of Rome. The opening shows that it does, though the rest of the play shows at what cost. Contradiction two: Cleopatra's detached and calculated mockery is a necessary yet finally unsatisfactory stimulant of Antony's rapture. In order to share that rapture, as Cleopatra does after Antony's death, Cleopatra must forego the mockery that provoked it. Contradiction three: The boundless love envisioned by Antony is expressed in the limited act of wandering

the streets. Only with time and defeat do the lovers learn that
they must lose the sensual delights of feast and flesh—the signs
of love—before they can gain the transcendence marked out in
the first lines. It is by subjecting these contradictions to the breaking point that Shakespeare refines the love so deliberately aroused
by Cleopatra and so facilely rhapsodized by Antony. The play
shows the irregular course of that refinement.

The second noteworthy feature is the kind of activity employed
to stimulate the structure just described. As we have seen, the
lovers are interrupted by one messenger announcing the arrival
of another messenger from Rome. This double use of messenger
is a foretaste of more to come. Messengers are not uncommon in
Shakespeare, of course, and they have appeared in drama since
the days of the Greeks. What is somewhat unusual, however, is
the number of messengers Shakespeare brings on stage in this
play. The double appearance in the first scene merely emphasizes their importance in *Antony and Cleopatra*. And yet we
should not speak of messengers as generic types. Far more important is to direct our attention to the messenger sequences that
abound. There are no less than thirty-five examples. In virtually
every scene someone plays messenger, and so prevalent is the
activity of delivering a message that this activity sets the rhythm
for the manifold motions of the play.

In *Antony and Cleopatra* the messenger sequence is so constructed that a messenger or a minor character or even occasionally a major character delivers a report to another figure. Clearly,
the report is crucial for the person who receives it. More important dramatically, however, is that only in a few instances does
the message contain information that is wholly new for the audience.[2] In most sequences the audience is already aware of the
news the messenger brings, as for instance in Act II, scene i when
one of Pompey's men, Varrius, tells Pompey that Antony is expected in Rome. Since the audience already has this information,
its attention is being clearly directed to Pompey's response.
Similar cases occur throughout the play. Sequences are structured
not to reveal what happens off stage, as so often occurs in Greek
tragedy, but to stimulate a response from one of the major
characters.

[2]Such messages are delivered early in the play: I.ii.115-118 on Fulvia's death;
I.iv.33-54 on the victories of Pompey and the sea pirates.

The responses of these characters are of two types: I will call one active and the other reactive. An active response is one that is intended to achieve a specific objective, as in giving a command. When a soldier reports to Caesar that "Antony/ Is come into the field" (IV.vi.7-8), Caesar immediately orders his troops into action. In this case his energy is directed toward a particular result. It is intended to affect others and thus is projected externally. The reactive response, on the other hand, lacks a specific goal. Instead, in responding to a messenger the character passes through a period of mental or emotional adjustment, as Antony does in Act I, scene ii. Upon hearing the report of the death of his first wife, Fulvia, he sends the messenger away and then says,

> There's a great spirit gone! Thus did I desire it:
> What our contempts doth often hurl from us,
> We wish it ours again. The present pleasure,
> By revolution lowering, does become
> The opposite of itself: she's good, being gone,
> The hand could pluck her back that shov'd her on.
>
> (119-124)

This reactive response then yields to an impulse that will later become active:

> I must from this enchanting queen break off.
>
> (125)

As we see here, Antony's energy is directed inward. It forces him to adjust to the report and work through his unsettled state. And as he passes through that unsettled state, we can perceive the subtle motions of thought and feeling which mark Antony and infuse the entire play.

These two types of responses: active and reactive, especially as they are sparked by the hordes of messengers, help to shape the rhythm of the play as well as define the characters. Caesar, for example, has a simple response to his messengers. It is usually active, but even when it is reactive, it is uniform. That is, the response is solely active or reactive in character. It does not alternate from one impulse to the other. Antony, on the other hand, often shifts from active to reactive impulse during the same sequence. On hearing of Enobarbus' desertion, he immediately commands Enobarbus' treasure to be sent to him. This is an active impulse. Then he laments, "O, my fortunes have/ Cor-

rupted honest men!" This is reactive. The next word is, "Despatch,"
that is, quickly send the treasure to Enobarbus. This is clearly
active. It is followed by another reactive lament of one word,
"Enobarbus." Thus the lines: O, my fortunes have/ Corrupted
honest men! Despatch.—Enobarbus" (IV.v.16-17) contain alternate shifts of energy, first reactive, then active, then reactive. Such
a rhythm communicates Antony's complexity and instability.

Naturally, the varying energies in the active and reactive
patterns contribute to our sense of each character's personality.
The contrast between energies is the main method by which
Caesar's cool steadiness is set against Antony's irresolution and
Cleopatra's famed variety. But these differing responses are even
more central to the experience that the play produces. Together
they embody the very forces that give shape to the action. Matched
against the calculating sureness of Caesar, the impulsive shifting
energies of Antony and Cleopatra follow an irregular course. It is
that course upon which our attention becomes fixed. We are
dazzled by its unpredictability and vitality. At the same time its
waywardness prevents us—at first, anyway—from becoming
emotionally engaged.

This course of fluctuating energies, however, does not unwind
in a void. The messenger sequences and the responses to them
provide a vibrant and crucial context, a context without example
in Plutarch. By employing messengers so profusely Shakespeare
causes the major figures to deal with each other through inter-
mediaries. This has the result of isolating them and thus makes
overcoming the isolation a principal action in the play. In addition, the comings and goings of messengers emphasize the fundamental instability of the situations in which the characters find
themselves. They can be disturbed at any moment. Isolation and
interruption thus permeate the play; in essence, they are the
obstacles Antony and Cleopatra must overcome. Isolation is not
mere separation, however. There is a deep-seated division between the two major characters that needs to be bridged. Only as
traces of an unwavering attachment to each other begin to appear
do we feel moved by the lovers.

Until this point I have shown how Shakespeare introduces
action patterns in the first scene that he varies and develops
throughout the play. These patterns define the relationships to
be explored, determine the scope of the events, and prefigure

the modes of action. As a result, the first scene is actually a pro-
logue that not only introduces the argument of the play but also
summarizes how it will proceed. What I find of especial significance is how Shakespeare deliberately limits his use of materials.
The messenger sequence is a case in point. Its frequency demon-
strates the tremendous variety with which Shakespeare employs
this activity, and at the same time its recurrence emphasizes with
what a restricted palette Shakespeare paints his action. He does
not rely on a wide range of activities, but is content to modulate
the tension that he introduces early in the play. By dramatizing
the essential issues in the first scene, he directs our attention both
to the issues and their manner of development. These issues in-
volve Cleopatra's effort to manipulate Antony and Antony's capacity to create a sustaining love. Related to these two motifs is
another one raised by the Roman soldiers at the end of scene i:
what is Antony's true self? The issues are worked out in the context of isolation and interruption that the messengers establish.
The backdrop of worldwide conflict and mythic figures lends a
poignancy to the context, but the true centers of interest are not
in the large motions of war and politics, but in the subtle jockeying
that goes on between the main characters.

How subtly and economically Shakespeare develops his action
can be seen in two later sequences involving Cleopatra. These
occur while Antony is in Rome, the first in Act I, scene v; the
second in Act II, scene v. Both are brief; both come immediately
prior to the entrance of a messenger, in the first sequence just
before the messenger comes to describe Antony's departure for
Rome, in the second sequence just before the messenger arrives
with word of Antony's marriage to Octavia. Both sequences have
identical structures. They each have a structure composed of
three segments. Each begins as Cleopatra longs for a drug, either
mandragora or music, in order to while away the days until
Antony returns. This is followed by Cleopatra's banter with the
eunuch Mardian in which she mocks him for his sexual incapacity.
Finally, Cleopatra abruptly returns to thoughts of Antony. It is
here that a significant variation occurs, for in the first sequence
her thinking of Antony leads her to remember how she con-
quered Julius Caesar and Pompey before him, thus making
Antony only the most recent victim of her charms. "Now I feed
myself/ With most delicious poison," she says:

> Think on me,
> That am with Phoebus' amorous pinches black,
> And wrinkled deep in time. Broad-fronted Caesar,
> When thou wast here above the ground, I was
> A morsel for a monarch: and great Pompey
> Would stand and make his eyes grow in my brow,
> There would he anchor his aspect, and die
> With looking on his life.   (I.v. 26-34)

The time between the first and second sequence suggests an historical progression as Cleopatra moves from remembrance of old
lovers to recollection of the new one. In the second sequence
she recalls amusing and teasing Antony, the climax of this memory coming when she delights in the power she exerted over him
by getting him to put on her dresses and mantles, "whilst," she
crows, "I wore his sword Philippan" (II.v.22-23). In short, her
image of shared love is to recall her partner transformed into a
woman and herself possessed of the very sword of victory with
which Antony defeated Brutus and Cassius.

   This image is a manifestation of the control that we saw Cleopatra attempt to exercise over Antony in the first scene. It is the
fullest expression of one side of her love, that side which can
undermine Antony's true self. By utilizing these parallel sequences, Shakespeare shows the persistence of Cleopatra's way of love
at the same time he reveals her restlessness.

   The persistence of Cleopatra's love image acts as a counter-
point to Antony's effort in Rome to assert his political position.
Yet even as he tries to do so, he knows that he can no longer look
at life through Roman eyes. Well before his marriage to Octavia,
he decides to return to Egypt (II.iii). Even as he negotiates and
parlays with Caesar and Pompey, his activities and the effect they
have on the others only serve to remind everyone of Egypt and
make its attraction more palpable. For despite the supposed
contrast between Rome and Egypt, we find that the aura of the
East permeates the Roman scenes. In the first one (I.iv) we hear
Octavius calling out to Antony to return; in the second (II.i)
Pompey calling out to Cleopatra to "tie up the libertine in a field
of feasts (23)"; in the third, after the parley, we listen to Enobarbus praising Cleopatra (II.ii); and near the end of the first half
of the play we witness the re-creation of an Egyptian dance on
Pompey's galley (II.vii). This drunken and unloosed merri-

ment is the ultimate point Antony reaches in juggling the things of Rome and the things of Egypt.

It is in the second half of the play, however, after Antony returns to Egypt, that the clash between Cleopatra's image of love and Antony's comes to a head. Until their defeat, their restless love lacks any sign of stability or continuity. For Antony it is a compulsion, for Cleopatra a challenge and necessity. Only after the naval disaster at Actium does the indication of a deeper relationship emerge. They are brought together by their attendants. Mournfully, Antony accuses Cleopatra of leading him to dishonour. "O'er my spirit/ Thy full supremacy thou knew'st, and that/ Thy beck might from the bidding of the gods/ Command me" (III.xi.58-61). She does not argue. "O, my pardon!" she murmurs. He imagines the shame he is now forced to face, of submitting himself to Caesar, and then turns on Cleopatra again:

> You did know
> How much you were my conqueror, and that
> My sword, made weak by my affection, would
> Obey it on all cause.   (65-68)

"Pardon, pardon!" she pleads. For the first time but one[3] Cleopatra appears divested of all calculation. For a moment, together they experience unaffected love. "Fall not a tear," Antony says, "one of them rates/ All that is won and lost: give me a kiss," and the kiss they exchange is one of reconciliation. "Even this repays me," Antony sighs.

But the mood lasts only an instant. Immediately, Antony calls for the messenger he had sent to Caesar.

> We sent our schoolmaster,
> Is 'a come back? Love, I am full of lead:
> Some wine within there, and our viands! Fortune knows,
> We scorn her most, when most she offers blows.
>   (71-74)

This passage follows the patterns of shifting from active, to reactive, to active again, and so returns them to their restless state.

The kiss they exchange in this scene is another echo of the first scene. It is a cousin to the one Antony gives Cleopatra when he

---

[3]One may regard Cleopatra's forgetfulness while bidding Antony farewell ("O, my oblivion is a very Antony") as a symptom of genuine feeling (I. iii. 90).

tells her, "The nobleness of life/ Is to do thus" (I.i.36-37). Although editors often add a stage direction to this line indicating that the lovers embrace, there is no authority for the gesture. The two may very well kiss, and a kiss, by comparison, is of far greater importance in the play, for kissing assumes dramatic significance in the second half.

In the scene following the naval disaster that I just cited, the kiss appears for the first time as a mark of tenderness, not lust. Later in Act III (xiii.81ff.), it is the kiss that Caesar's messenger Thidias places on Cleopatra's hand that enrages Antony because he regards it as a sign of disloyalty and lust. And in Act IV, scene viii, Antony rewards one of his lieutenants with an identical kiss. There it is a sign of worthiness and loyalty. By the time Antony lies dying, the kiss has become a mark of spiritual union, as we shall see. I cite the various contexts of the kisses because their significance to the progression of the play outweighs their rarity. The kiss between Antony and Cleopatra after the naval disaster thus initiates those moments of unaffected tenderness in which each lover is at peace with the other. These moments grow in dramatic power during the fourth and fifth acts, and become the main counterweight to the impulses toward isolation and interruption. But unfortunately they are only moments. They are caught in the flurry of events. They run counter to the flamboyant lovemaking of Antony and Cleopatra. That is why they appear fleetingly and are so often overlooked, and that is why they often have a dreamlike quality.

When after fantasizing that he will join her in Elysium, Antony is brought to Cleopatra's monument (IV.xv), the dream might be expected to take on substance. The time seems ripe for the full expression of their love. But their close contact lasts only for the span of a kiss, for she lapses into railing against fortune and he gives her political advice. Thus their only genuine harmony is that last kiss, a long one taken to the chorus of "a heavy sight" (40). After he dies, her lament, "O withered is the garland of the war" (64) more eloquently expresses her union with him than anything she says as he lies dying. Moments like these, Cleopatra's "pardon, pardon," their rare kisses, and her brief elegy convey a sense of spiritual union. These are rare instances when neither the active nor reactive energies are in motion, but instead an impression of absolute stillness is created.

Only in the last scene before her death does Cleopatra reach a complete state of spiritual identity with Antony. As prefigured in the first scene, his sense of love prevails. No longer does she need to emasculate him. She accepts him as he shaped himself during the last half of the play. Because their union was always so fragile, however, she experiences this union more as a dream than a reality, or a reality that has the substance of a dream, just as Antony did. "I dreamt there was an Emperor Antony," she says (V.ii.76), and then conjures up an image of a demi-god. What she evokes is that still reality toward which their love moved, and even though she bargains with Caesar and thus exhibits her old habits, the image of Antony ultimately prevails.

But is her dream of Antony hollow? Is he the demi-god she imagines? After all his failures as a soldier, can we share her estimation of him? Again, it is through one of those subtle revelations that Shakespeare shows us an Antony redeemed. During the fourth act Antony mounts in stature, not as a soldier, but as a man in relationship to other men. This becomes evident in act IV, scene vii. Antony has just fought one of those minor scuffles by which he holds off defeat momentarily. He returns victorious, but shows none of his former excess of emotion or changeability. It is his follower Scarus who boasts of their success. Antony himself speaks only a few words. He is concerned about Scarus' wounds, he observes that Caesar's soldiers withdraw, he thinks of rewarding his men. It is right after this moment that he gives Scarus the unmatchable joy of kissing Cleopatra's hand. And indeed, the fourth act is filled with Antony's acts of generosity, not only to Scarus but to his men at large. So, after scenes of self-pity and egotistical vaunting, Antony achieves a selflessness. It is for such a man that Eros slays himself and Enobarbus pines away, and it is such a man who justifies Cleopatra's dream.

As I see it then, the subtle motions of the play dramatize the growth of the still moments of communion in the teeth of the unstable shifts of will, passion, and calculation with which Antony and Cleopatra habitually meet the world. Because of this action, the scale of production must not be, as it invariably is, spectacular. The moments between Antony and Cleopatra, moments that hint at a transcendent devotion, are so fragile, so evanescent that they must be nurtured tenderly. Nor is the actor's task merely to make us cognizant of these moments. He must project them so that they affect us deeply, so that they assume such vivid life that they finally become the prevailing sense of the play. For what Shakespeare has created is not a symphony, but a chamber work. Great events occur. But they strike us by refraction. We are in the anteroom for the most part, not where great parlays are held but where private realization occurs. We receive the messengers who carry on the business of tying the world together, but we ourselves are left to ponder the messages. And therefore a certain intimacy, a certain nearness between the audience and characters is necessary. The spectacle of Antony's and Cleopatra's defeat as kings interests us but little. Their painful struggle to touch each other truly is what finally holds our attention.

Not that Antony and Cleopatra's positions as rulers can be ignored. Both exist in a world where they must use political power. They, however, want more than naked power. Sensual satisfaction, restless and fickle, appears to be the only alternative. In such a world luxury and sexual fulfillment are often confused with politics on the one hand and love on the other. Against power and seduction, human contact of a spiritual nature is hard to sustain. Even when moments of a true intimacy occur, these quickly slip away. Shakespeare seems to indicate that Antony and Cleopatra—and perhaps we—can dream and occasionally touch this true intimacy, but perhaps can never live it fully.

PART THREE

View Points

George Bernard Shaw: The Tragedy of Infatuation

The very name of Cleopatra suggests at once a tragedy of Circe, with the horrible difference that whereas the ancient myth rightly represents Circe as turning heroes into hogs, the modern romantic convention would represent her as turning hogs into heroes. Shakespeare's *Antony and Cleopatra* must needs be as intolerable to the true Puritan as it is vaguely distressing to the ordinary healthy citizen, because, after giving a faithful picture of the soldier broken down by debauchery, and the typical wanton in whose arms such men perish, Shakespeare finally strains all his huge command of rhetoric and stage pathos to give a theatrical sublimity to the wretched end of the business, and to persuade foolish spectators that the world was well lost by the twain. Such falsehood is not to be borne except by the real Cleopatras and Antonys (they are to be found in every public house) who would no doubt be glad enough to be transfigured by some poet as immortal lovers. Woe to the poet who stoops to such folly! The lot of the man who sees life truly and thinks about it romantically is Despair. How well we know the cries of that despair! Vanity of vanities, all is vanity! moans the Preacher, when life has at last taught him that Nature will not dance to his moralist-made tunes. Thackeray, scores of centuries later, was still baying at the moon in the same terms. Out, out, brief candle! cries Shakespeare, in his tragedy of the modern literary man as murderer and witch consulter. Surely the time is past for patience with writers who, having to choose between giving up life in despair and discarding the trumpery moral kitchen scales in which they try to weigh the universe, superstitiously stick to the scales, and spend the rest of the lives they pretend to despise in breaking men's spirits. But even in pessimism there is a choice between intellectual honesty and dishonesty. Hogarth drew the rake and the harlot without glorifying their end. Swift, accepting our system of morals and religion, delivered the inevitable ver-

"The Tragedy of Infatuation" (Editor's title). From *Prefaces by Bernard Shaw* (London: Constable and Company Ltd., 1934), pp. 716-17. Reprinted by permission of The Society of Authors on behalf of the Bernard Shaw Estate.

dict of that system on us through the mouth of the king of Brobdingnag, and described Man as the Yahoo, shocking his superior the horse by his every action. Strindberg, the only genuinely Shakespearean modern dramatist, shows that the female Yahoo, measured by romantic standards, is viler than her male dupe and slave. I respect these resolute tragi-comedians: they are logical and faithful: they force you to face the fact that you must either accept their conclusions as valid (in which case it is cowardly to continue living) or admit that their way of judging conduct is absurd. But when your Shakespeares and Thackerays huddle up the matter at the end by killing somebody and covering your eyes with the undertaker's handkerchief, duly onioned with some pathetic phrase, as The flight of angels sing thee to thy rest, or Adsum, or the like, I have no respect for them at all: such maudlin tricks may impose on tea-drunkards, not on me.

Besides, I have a technical objection to making sexual infatuation a tragic theme. Experience proves that it is only effective in the comic spirit. We can bear to see Mrs. Quickly pawning her plate for love of Falstaff, but not Antony running away from the battle of Actium for love of Cleopatra. Let realism have its demonstration, comedy its criticism, or even bawdry its horse-laugh at the expense of sexual infatuation, if it must; but to ask us to subject our souls to its ruinous glamor, to worship it, deify it, and imply that it alone makes our life worth living, is nothing but folly gone mad erotically—a thing compared to which Falstaff's unbeglamored drinking and drabbing is respectable and rightminded....

Northrop Frye: The Tailors of the Earth:
The Tragedy of Passion

Antony and Cleopatra is the definitive tragedy of passion, and in it the ironic and heroic themes, the day world of history and the night world of passion, expand into natural forces of cosmological proportions. The Western and Roman world is per-

"The Tailors of the Earth: The Tragedy of Passion." From *Fools of Time: Studies in Shakespearean Tragedy,* by Northrop Frye (Toronto: University of Toronto Press, 1967), pp. 70-74. © University of Toronto Press, 1967. Reprinted by permission of University of Toronto Press.

vaded by order, rule, and measure: when Antony tries to live by
its standards he says:

> I have not kept my square; but that to come
> Shall all be done by th' rule.

Its commander is Octavius Caesar, the very incarnation of history
and the world's greatest order-figure, a leader who is ruthless yet
not really treacherous given the conditions of a ruler's task, who
is always provided with all the justifications he needs for des-
troying Antony. Here, turning the wheel of history appears in its
most persuasive form as conquering the world, and conquering
the world, being thought of as ultimately the most real activity,
is presented as a duty. It has many moral imperatives on its side,
but we can hardly say that it is a pattern of virtue, at least so far
as it affects Antony. As a Roman soldier, Antony reminds us more
of the Antony in *Julius Caesar,* an altogether smaller character.
His lieutenant Ventidius, in a highly significant speech, alludes
to the danger of a subordinate's doing so well as to affect his
superior's "image," as we would say now. Antony is much more
calculating, when doing his conquering duty, than he is when he
rewards the deserting Enobarbus, or when he turns the con-
ference on Pompey's ship into an epiphany of Dionysus.

The eastern and Egyptian world is presided over by Cleopatra,
queen of the ancient and timeless land which renews its fertility
by the overflowing of the Nile each year. The play opens with
the remark that Antony's dotage "O'erflows the measure," which
is a Roman view, and Cleopatra's world is a Dionysian world of
gigantic feasting and drunkenness and love-making. Both worlds
are equally hard on the taxpayer, to use a standard that Plutarch
at least is aware of even if Shakespeare ignores it. Each world is a
self-evident reality to itself and an illusion to its rival. To the
Romans, Antony is "not Antony" in Egypt: to Cleopatra, if he
stays there, he "will be himself." Antony himself, of course, tends
to find his identity in his immediate context, and to waver disas-
trously between the two. But just as Octavius is the incarnation of
history, so Cleopatra, like Falstaff, is a counter-historical figure.
Most of what she substitutes for heroic action is idleness and
distraction, and there is plenty of textual justification for making
her a straight temptress like the other Renaissance sirens who

entice the hero from his quest with some Bower of Bliss or lotus land. The Egypt of the play includes the Biblical Egypt, the land of bondage, and the Egypt of legend in which serpents and crocodiles are spawned from the mud of the Nile. Cleopatra, the serpent of the Nile, is a Venus rising from it in Enobarbus' speech; she wears the regalia of Isis; she is a *stella maris,* a goddess of the moon and the sea. She has affinities with the kind of goddess figure that both Hebraic and Classical religions kept trying to subdue by abuse: she is a whore and her children are all bastards; she is a snare to men and destroys their masculinity, making them degenerate slaves like Circe; she is an Omphale dressing her Hercules in women's clothes; she has many characteristics of her sister whore of Babylon. This last gives a curiously apocalyptic tone to the play: just as *Troilus and Cressida* is something of a secular fall, so *Antony and Cleopatra,* with its references to "Herod of Jewry," seems a kind of summing up of the old dispensation. The final cadences of the play seem to unite the two Biblical demonic themes, Egypt and the serpent, in a way that makes Cleopatra a central symbol of everything sinister in human history:

> This is an aspic's trail: and these fig-leaves
> Have slime upon them, such as the aspic leaves
> Upon the caves of Nile.

But *Antony and Cleopatra* is not a morality play, and Egypt is not hell: it is rather the night side of nature, passionate, cruel, superstitious, barbaric, dissolute, what you will, but not to be identified with its vices, any more than Rome can be identified with its virtues. Prince Henry finds himself in the same Dionysian night world when he is a youth, and still has the choice of going up the wheel of fortune and history or of plunging downward into a world which becomes with increasing clarity a world of thieves and whores. But Henry, like Odin in the Eddas, learns a good deal from his descent and escapes from it at the sacrifice of some of his humanity. Antony is on the other side of the wheel: he can only fall out of history and action into the anti-historical and mythical world of passion opposite it, where the dominating figure is female and the hero is her subordinate. The slighter and younger Octavius goes up the wheel and takes command of history: Antony goes to a hero's destruction, yet even in his death he is upstaged by Cleopatra, who monopolizes the attention of the audience to the end, looking in her death ready to "catch another Antony" and start all over. She is worth the attention, because she is all we can see of a world as big as the Roman world, and not only all we can see of it but that world in herself, a microcosm of passion "whom everything becomes." Her Egypt is able to bring a super-human vitality out of Antony that Rome cannot equal, not in spite of the fact that it destroys him, but because it destroys him.

At the close of the play the two ends of the wheel confront each other: the Cleopatra who has

> pursued conclusions infinite
> Of easy ways to die

and the Caesar who has been equally busy in pursuing difficult ways to live. Rome with its measure and order has won out over the overflowing Nile: the last line of the play urges us, in Caesar's voice, to see "High order in this great solemnity." But we can see something else besides high order: we can see that there is a part of nature that can never be ordered, a colossal exuberance of powers, the tailors of the earth as Enobarbus calls them, that weave and unweave the forms of life. Antony has caught a glimpse of these powers at the price of disappearing like a cloud when "the rack dislimns," for it is only a self-destroying will that can bring one close to them. In fact Antony may say, with Slender in *The Merry Wives*, "I am freely dissolved, and dissolutely." Hercules has deserted him, but we remember how Hercules got rid of the burden of the world by tricking Atlas into re-assuming it: perhaps there is something gullible about Caesar, as Cleopatra suggests when she says she hears Antony

> mock
> The luck of Caesar, which the gods give men
> To excuse their after wrath.

However, Caesar is now the master of his world, the secular counterpart to Christ, the off-stage presence in *Cymbeline* who is able to exact tribute from the end of the world in Britain even when defeated there. We say, in Roman terms, that Antony has lost "the world" for love. But his disappearance from that world is also, in a final twist of the tragic paradox, the appearance of another world that endures no master.

Janet Adelman: Character and Knowledge

Although the play continually raises questions about motives, it simply does not give any clear answers to them. Almost every major action in the play is in some degree inexplicable. Why did Antony marry Octavia if he planned to return to Cleopatra? Was Octavius ruthless or merely blind in his plan to marry his sister to Antony? Does Antony return to the East for love of Cleopatra or because his spirit is overpowered when he is near Octavius? As the play progresses, the questions accumulate around Cleopatra; and they become more urgent. Is Cleopatra merely exercising her powers over Thidias for the sake of the game, or does she really hope to woo Octavius through him? Is her scene with Seleucus a cunningly staged device to convince Octavius that she has no desire to die, or does she in fact have hopes of a future life without Antony in which some lady trifles will be useful? Even the most critical action in the plot goes unexplained: Antony has won a victory against Octavius and regained the loyalty of his own men (a victory greatly magnified in importance from the account in Plutarch); but in the next encounter, his fleet yields to Octavius and his defeat is certain. Did the ships join with Octavius under Cleopatra's orders, as Antony assumes? If not, then who is responsible for this final betrayal of Antony? These questions are not all equally unanswerable; and our preferences and critical ingenuity will usually combine with the text of the play to produce satisfactory answers to most of them. But most of the time the answers will satisfy only ourselves. I for one am as unwilling to imagine a fundamentally disloyal Cleopatra as the most romantic critic and will argue for the best possible interpretation of her actions; but the fact is that the play will support the arguments of my opponents almost as readily as mine. We simply are not told the motives of the protagonists at the most critical points in the action.

Shakespeare was not accustomed to leaving his audience entirely in the dark on central issues in his tragedies. We may not know why Lear chooses to divide his kingdom so arbitrarily; but

"Character and Knowledge." From *The Common Liar: An Essay on "Antony and Cleopatra,"* by Janet Adelman (New Haven and London: Yale University Press, 1973), pp. 15–24. Copyright © 1973 by Yale University Press. Reprinted, with the deletion of the original footnotes, by permission of the author and Yale University Press.

once we have accepted the initial situation, we are given frequent
insights into his mind through his own soliloquies and asides and
through a technique of projection called "umbrella speeches"
by Maynard Mack, in which the fool, for instance, serves "as a
screen on which Shakespeare flashes, as it were, readings from
the psychic life of the protagonists." But in *Antony and Cleopatra,* the only major soliloquy is Enobarbus's; and the asides are
almost exclusively the property of the minor characters. Antony
does tell us in soliloquy of his determination to return to the East
(2.3) and of his rage and love for Cleopatra (4.12; 4.14); but these
speeches are by no means the meditations on his own inner state
which we associate with soliloquy in the major tragedies. Moreover, the "umbrella speeches" and speeches by other characters
which seem to reflect the state of the protagonists accurately often
turn out upon examination to be wrong. No play in which the
characters remain so essentially opaque to each other and to the
audience can satisfy us in the way of *Macbeth*—in the way, that is,
of character revelation and moral certainty.

There are, of course, moments at which the characters are
opaque in the other tragedies, but these mysteries are, I think, of
a slightly different order. Generations of critics have argued, for
instance, about why Hamlet does not kill the king while he is
praying. Is it really because he does not want to send Claudius's
soul to heaven, or must we look deeper into Hamlet's character
toward those philosophic or psychoanalytic scruples which keep
him from action altogether? We must note that Hamlet himself
gives us a perfectly good reason for not killing Claudius praying:
that heaven is no recompense for hell. Although we may choose
(at our peril) to disbelieve his reason, it is at any rate evident that
Hamlet believes it. Moreover, we are informed at this critical
moment of the process of Hamlet's mind: although we may feel
that we have not been told the whole truth, at least the illusion of
insight into Hamlet's motivation has been given by the soliloquy.
If an aura of mystery persists nonetheless, it is perhaps because
the literary figure in this instance creates so absolute an illusion
of reality that he breeds all the mysteries of character which we
find in real life. The sense of opaqueness comes more from the
success of the illusion than from any failure to explicate character: Shakespeare gives us insight into Hamlet's inner state at
virtually every turn in the play.

A fully realized character like Hamlet will necessarily appear

mysterious at some moments precisely insofar as he is fully
realized; a relatively unrealized character like Iago will engender
mysteries of another sort. Iago's frequent soliloquies reveal his
motives and his machinations: Cassio has got the job he wanted;
he suspects both Cassio and Othello of cuckholding him; and the
daily beauty of Cassio's life makes his own ugly. But the more
motives Iago gives us, the less likely they seem as explanations
of his actions. His motives do not seem equal to the deed, nor can
they account for that fundamental hatred of life and love of con-
trivance which rule him. "I hate the Moor," he says, and then
explicitly denies that he hates him for any particular reason:

> And it is thought abroad, that 'twixt my sheets
> He's done my office; I know not if't be true…
> Yet I, for mere suspicion in that kind,
> Will do, as if for surety.   (1.3.385-388)

We are not here fundamentally concerned with Iago's character;
mere ordinary human motivation is serving as the excuse for
some more essential hatred which it surely could not have caused.
Our impression, despite the soliloquies and their revelation of
motivation, is not that the byways of Iago's character have been
revealed to us but rather that essential evil of Iago's sort is a self-
perpetuating, self-aggrandizing, and finally self-annihilating
machine to which motivation is almost wholly irrelevant after
the initial move is made. We become more interested in watch-
ing the diabolical principle at work in a human being than in
the character of Iago per se and his inconsistent motivation. It is
with a similar disinterest in the intricacies of character that we
watch the redemptive principle working through Cordelia.
Figures like Iago or Cordelia tend to function less as fully realized
characters than as embodiments of moral principles. And in proportion as they are less fully human than Hamlet, as they are
more purely symbolic, we are less interested in their inner states.
They can afford to be opaque because we are not fundamentally
interested in them as characters: mysteries of motivation simply
evaporate insofar as they take their places as parts of a symbolic
action.

But in *Antony and Cleopatra*, the protagonists neither reveal
their motives to us nor are they content merely to take their places
in a symbolic action. They create the same sort of illusion of reality

that Hamlet creates but do not give us even the partial insights into their souls that Hamlet gives. We are forced to concern ourselves with their characters as we are not with Iago's or Cordelia's; and yet their characters remain opaque. True, a desire to understand character in the play may be dismissed by some modern critics as naïve; and there is little question that *Antony and Cleopatra* becomes a more unified and explicable whole if it is read as a lyric poem or an allegory to which questions of character are largely irrelevant. But we may not be able to believe entirely in the play-as-lyric-poem of Knight and Knights or in the character-as-a-bundle-of-stage-conventions of Schücking and Stoll or in the character-as-symbol of Bethell; or at least these theories may not be able to explain away character altogether. However convincing they are in part, they do not quite allay the nagging suspicion that the illusion of character is in some measure relevant to drama, and particularly to this one. Critics have persisted in trying to find answers to the questions of motivation and emotion in *Antony and Cleopatra;* and though questions of character may occasionally be irrelevant, this critical persistence suggests that they are not irrelevant here. If the same questions are continually asked, then I think we must conclude that the questions have been elicited by the play; the search is interminable not because the questions are wrong but because the answers are not given.

To explain character away, and with it the unanswerable questions, is in this instance to explain the play away: for the whole play can be seen as a series of attempts on the parts of the characters to understand and judge each other and themselves. We see Cleopatra dallying with Thidias in act 3, scene 13: Enobarbus thinks he sees Cleopatra betraying Antony and transferring her allegiance to Caesar; Antony thinks he sees the operations of lascivious habit. What have they seen? Do we watch a cunning queen outfox a wily politician in the scene with Seleucus, or a servant betray his mistress? This uncertainty is apparent not only in the critical moments of the play (did Cleopatra's ships join Caesar's on her orders?) but during numerous small scenes. And we are as baffled as the characters; like them, we see only the bare event and are left to speculate upon its meaning.

Throughout the play, the characters themselves question its meaning for us; the questioning is so habitual that it occurs explicitly even in those relatively minor scenes where the meaning does not seem to be at issue. When the soothsayer tells Charmian that she shall be far fairer than she is, the two women debate his meaning:

> *Char.* He means in flesh.
> *Iras.* No, you shall paint when you are old.
>   (1.2.17-18)

Their debate is poignant because neither can guess the true meaning of his prophecies. The question of meaning is most explicitly raised in the small scene in which Antony bids his servants farewell; there it is raised four times in thirty-five lines. We would expect Cleopatra to know Antony as well as anyone; yet she asks Enobarbus, "What means this?" (4.2.13) and, ten lines later, "What does he mean?" Enobarbus then asks Antony directly: "What mean you, sir,/ To give them this discomfort?" (lines 33-34). Antony immediately denies that he meant his words as Enobarbus and the servants have taken them:

> Ho, ho, ho!
> Now the witch take me, if I meant it thus!
> Grace grow where those drops fall, my hearty friends;
> You take me in too dolorous a sense,
> For I spake to you for your comfort.   (4.2.36-40)

Antony's attempt to console his followers by rearranging his meaning explicitly raises the issue of interpretation; even here, we are faced with one of the central dilemmas of the play. Virtually the only way out of this dilemma is the way that Antony takes at the end of the scene, when he in effect plays Horatio to his own Hamlet: "Let's to supper, come,/ And drown consideration" (lines 44-45). In the scene which follows immediately, we are shown another farewell embedded in controversy:

> *Sec. Sold.* Heard you of nothing strange about the streets?
> *First Sold.* Nothing: what news?
> *Sec. Sold.* Belike 'tis but a rumour.   (4.3.3-5)

The rumor is of course instantly verified: the music of Hercules departing is heard and debated.

> *Fourth Sold.* It signs well, does it not?
> *Third Sold.*   No.
> *First Sold.*   Peace, I say:
>   What should this mean?

> *Sec. Sold.*   'Tis the god Hercules, whom Antony lov'd,
>   Now leaves him.   (4.3.13-16)

Nothing goes unquestioned in this play. In most literature
there is a convention that character is knowable as it rarely is in
life, that characters act in accordance with certain constant,
recognizable, and explicable principles which we and they can
know. This convention does not operate in *Antony and Cleopatra*. There the characters do not know each other, nor can we
know them, any more clearly than we know ourselves. In the
midst of Antony's rage against Cleopatra and Thidias, Cleopatra
asks him, "Not know me yet?" (3.12.157). Antony can scarcely be
blamed for not knowing Cleopatra; the question stands as central
to the play. From Cleopatra's "If it be love indeed, tell me how
much" (1.1.14) to the First Guardsman's "Is this well done?"
(5.2.324), questions of motive, of value, and of the truth of the
emotions are insistently raised. Emotions are unreliable and
constantly changing; characters question their own emotions as
well as those of others. From the beginning we see Cleopatra stage
emotions for Antony's benefit ("If you find him sad,/ Say I am
dancing" 1.3.3-4; "I am sick, and sullen" 1.3.13). She accuses
Antony of playacting his rage ("You can do better yet; but this is
meetly" [1.3.81]. We know that Antony "married but his occasion"
(2.6.128) in marrying Octavia, for he himself tells us, "I make this
marriage for my peace" (2.3.38). But what of Fulvia? "Why did he
marry Fulvia, and not love her?" (1.1.41). Even Antony muses
on his inconstant emotions: "she's good, being gone,/ The hand
could pluck her back that shov'd her on" (1.2.123-124). Is Antony's
emotion love indeed? Cleopatra asks, "Why should I think you
can be mine and true.../ Who have been false to Fulvia?" (1.3.27-
29). Why indeed? Antony thinks Cleopatra's passions are feigned:
"She is cunning past man's thought" (1.2.143). But Enobarbus
answers that "her passions are made of nothing but the finest
parts of pure love" (1.2.144-145); and whatever his tone of voice,
his words at least contradict Antony's. Enobarbus and Agrippa
mock Lepidus's protestations of love for both Antony and Caesar
(3.2). Cleopatra idly asks, "Did I, Charmian,/ Ever love Caesar
so?" (1.5.66-67), and is most displeased with Charmian's teasing
answer.

The tears wept by Antony's crocodile are characteristic of this
persistent questioning of emotion. Cleopatra assumes that Antony

will weep crocodile tears for her: "I prithee turn aside and weep
for her,/ Then bid adieu to me, and say the tears/ Belong to
Egypt" (1.3.76-78). "The tears live in an onion, that should water
this sorrow" (1.2.167-168), Enobarbus says of Fulvia's death; yet
even when Enobarbus is genuinely moved by Antony's farewell
to his servants, he calls himself "onion-ey'd" (4.2.35). When
Caesar weeps at parting from Octavia, Agrippa recalls Antony's
tears:

> When Antony found Julius Caesar dead,
> He cried almost to roaring; and he wept
> When at Philippi he found Brutus slain.
>   (3.2.54-56)

Characteristically, Enobarbus points the moral:

> That year, indeed, he was troubled with a rheum;
> What willingly he did confound, he wail'd,
> Believe't, till I wept too.   (3.2.57-59)

Antony's weeping over Brutus recalls his sorrow over Fulvia; in
both instances he grieves for what he himself has helped to destroy. The movement is characteristic of the play: we shall see
Caesar too weep at what willingly he did confound when Decretas
reports Antony's death ("The gods rebuke me, but it is a tidings/
To wash the eyes of kings" [5.1.27-28]); Agrippa comments upon
the inconsistency of the emotion much as Enobarbus and Antony
have already commented ("And strange it is,/ That nature must
compel us to lament/ Our most persisted deeds" [5.1.28-30]). During Cleopatra's suicide, Charmian asks in effect for cosmic crocodile tears, for the show of cosmic grief: "Dissolve, thick cloud,
and rain, that I may say,/ The gods themselves do weep!" (5.2.298-
299).

The full acknowledgement of all this uncertainty is in Antony's
quiet lines, "I made these wars for Egypt, and the queen,/ Whose
heart I thought I had, for she had mine" (4.14.15-16). Does Antony
have her heart? Or does she too discover that Antony is good
only when he is gone? In the end, the uncertainty implicates us as
well as the characters: we must question Cleopatra's love for
Antony as she plans her suicide; Shakespeare's insistence upon
her dread of a Roman triumph forces us to question it. But in
this play, not even skepticism is a secure position: Enobarbus
shows us that. He persistently questions the sincerity of the pas-

sions, but when he follows his reason, he dies of a broken heart. At his death, we who have agreed with his rational skepticism are at a loss: skepticism itself is no more reliable than passion. If we are finally convinced of Cleopatra's love—and I think we are— we have had to develop a faith nearly as difficult as Antony's, a faith in what we cannot know.

Maynard Mack: Mobility and Mutability in *Antony and Cleopatra*

The "fall" story chiseled out of Plutarch receives in the finished play many kinds of imaginative extension, as every spectator will remember. One of these is the intricately elaborated context of mobility and mutability within which the fall is shown to occur, so that here as elsewhere in Shakespeare a play's characteristic "world" and its major action tend to become expressions of each other.

Our sense of a world in flux in *Antony and Cleopatra* is created primarily through the imagery, as many have pointed out, but in the theater it reaches us yet more directly through continual shifts of place (to mention only those of the first three acts: from Egypt to Rome to Egypt to Messina to Rome to Egypt to Misenum to Syria to Rome to Egypt to Athens to Rome to Actium to Egypt), and in the number and brevity of the episodes and scenes. In its episodic character, in fact, the play again seems mindful of the medieval past, each scene acted, as it were, from an appropriate historical "maison" or pageant-wagon, as in the cyclical plays. Today, the text of *Antony and Cleopatra* is usually divided into forty-two scenes, and while these need not be taken seriously as divisions of the action, since the folio text has neither scenes nor acts, their number indicates to us how often we are asked to register that one time, place, mood, or person gives way before another.

To this we must add the equally striking circumstance that *Antony and Cleopatra* in performance contains just under two

"Mobility and Mutability in *Antony and Cleopatra*" (Editor's title). From *"Antony and Cleopatra:* The Stillness and the Dance," by Maynard Mack, in *Shakespeare's Art: Seven Essays,* ed. Milton Crane (Chicago and London: The University of Chicago Press for The George Washington University, 1973), pp. 89-95. Copyright © 1973 by The George Washington University. Reprinted by permission of the author.

hundred distinct entrances and exits (rather more than one per minute of playing time) and that a great many of these acquire a special impact on our senses, either from being ceremonial and accompanied by much fanfare or from their effect in bringing about emotionally significant leave-takings and reunions. People flow to and away from each other in *Antony and Cleopatra* with relentless frequency and ease—Antony from Cleopatra and to her, to Caesar and from him; Octavia from Caesar and to him, to Antony and from him; Enobarbus from Antony, then (in heart) to him; and Cleopatra—who can say? This pattern is climaxed by the great reunions and leave-takings of the close. Antony, after being reunited with Cleopatra in her monument, takes his last farewell of her ("I am dying, Egypt, dying"); Cleopatra takes hers of Caesar and the world ("Give me my robe, put on my crown"); and both farewells are preludes, so the lovers insist, to a further reunion in the Elysian fields, or on the Cydnus, where the great passion will begin anew. Nothing seems to be granted finality in *Antony and Cleopatra,* perhaps not even death.

Mobility and mutability are not confined to spatial and geographical forms, but penetrate the play at every point. They are reiterated in the allusions to the ebbing and flowing of the tides; the rising and setting (or eclipse and extinction) of stars, moons, and suns; the immense reversals of feeling in the lovers and in Enobarbus; the career of Pompey, whose powers, "crescent" in II,i, are by III,v scattered and the man himself dead; and the steady erosion of persons whom for a moment we have known or heard of as presences: Fulvia, Lepidus, Pompey, Pacorus, Enobarbus, Alexas, and Eros all are dead before Antony dies; Menas and Menecrates, Philo and Demetrius, Ventidius and Scarus have disappeared without a trace, along with Mardian; Candidus and Decretas (besides Alexas and Enobarbus) have turned their coats, and Cleopatra may or may not have been several times on the verge of turning hers.

In addition, the style itself generates impressions of this kind. Johnson's account of the play rightly emphasizes the "hurry," the "quick succession" of events that calls the attention forward; and part of the effect he has in mind comes clearly from the style, which pours rather than broods (as in *Macbeth),* which is sensuous rather than intellectual (as in *Hamlet),* and which, as Pope said of Homer's, animates everything it touches: from Philo's view of

Antony in I,i, where eyes glow, bend, turn, and the heart remembers buckles it has burst in the scuffles of great fights, to Cleopatra's view of him in V,ii, where he bestrides, rears, crests; quails and shakes the orb with rattling thunder; gives in a perpetual autumn; sports like a dolphin above the ocean of his pleasure; and scatters crowns and coronets from his pockets as if they were small change.

Most striking of all, perhaps, is Shakespeare's use of the grammatical mood that, of all moods, best expresses mobility and mutability: the optative. Most of the great speeches in the play are "options"—in the radical sense. At all levels, high and low, playful and serious, hearts continually press forward with their longings, so much so that by placing even a few of them in sequence one may easily recapitulate the action.

Let Rome in Tiber melt.   (I.i.33)

Let me be married to three kings in a forenoon and widow them all....Find me to marry me with Octavius Caesar, and companion me with my mistress.   (I.ii.25-29)

Upon your sword
Sit laurel victory, and smooth success
Be strewed before your feet!
      (I.iii.99-101)

Let his shames quickly
Drive him to Rome.
      (I.iv.72-73)

But all the charms of love,
Salt Cleopatra, soften thy waned lip!
Let witchcraft join with beauty, lust with both!
      (II.i.20-22)

Let her live
To join our kingdoms and our hearts and never
Fly off our loves again.   (II.ii.151-153)

Would I had never come from thence, nor you thither.
      (II.iii.12)

Melt Egypt into Nile! and kindly creatures
Turn all to serpents!   (II.v.78-79)

In thy fats our cares be drowned,
With thy grapes our hairs be crowned.
(II.vii.114-115)

Sink Rome, and their tongues rot
That speak against us!   (III.vii.15-16)

O that I were
Upon the hill of Basan, to outroar
The horned herd!
(III.xiii.126-128)

This is a selection simply, and from the first three acts. There-
after, for obvious reasons, the optative mood quickens, to culminate at last in three of the best known utterances in the play:

We'll bury him; and then, what's brave, what's noble,
Let's do't after the high Roman fashion.
And make death proud to take us.   (IV.xv.89-91)

I dreamt there was an Emperor Antony.
O, such another sleep, that I might see
But such another man!   (V.ii.76-78)

Husband, I come:
Now to that name my courage prove my title!
(V.ii.286-287)

To all these impressions of a world in motion, much is added
in performance by the playwright's insistent stress on messages
and messengers—though here, doubtless, other effects and purposes must also receive their due. To ignore a man's messenger
who has a legitimate claim on you, as Antony does in I,i, or to
have such a messenger whipped, as he does in III,xiii, or, like
Cleopatra in II,v, to assault a messenger for the bad news he
carries: these are Shakespeare's equivalents in this play of Hamlet's melancholy, Lear's quick wrath—marks of the tragic person-
age's incapacity or unwillingness to adjust to the world he lives
in. Messengers also, of course, enhance our sense of power and
of the rearrangements that take place in power as the play wears
on. Cleopatra's inexhaustible supply of emissaries and her determination to "unpeople Egypt" (I.v.78) rather than let Antony in

Rome go a day without a letter bear testimony to her political stature at the outset of the play as well as to her passion. Later on, the fact that Antony, who has had "superfluous kings for messengers" (III.xii.5), is reduced to using his children's schoolmaster to carry a message to Caesar serves as an index to the audience as well as to Caesar that his wing has indeed been "plucked." Such effects are of course highly visual in performance, and capable in some contexts of communicating exquisite ironies. In the last scene, for instance, Caesar's messengers come and go again and again in a fine show of strategy and efficiency, but then comes the messenger no one anticipated, a bumpkin and malapropist bearing figs, who is escorted in by Caesar's own guard; and he proves to be the messenger that counts.

Beyond this, the play's emphasis on messengers reminds us that, in so volatile and mutable a world, opinion and report are matters of huge concern. All these people have an immense curiosity about each other, especially the Romans about Cleopatra, which they can only satisfy with fresh news. "From Alexandria," says Caesar to Lepidus the first time we see him, "This is the news" (I.iv.3-4), and he goes on to detail Antony's ill courses there. After the triumvirs have made peace in Rome, Enobarbus is no sooner left alone with Maecenas and Agrippa than they throw out bait about life in Egypt that they hope he will rise to: "Eight wild-boars roasted whole at a breakfast, and but twelve persons there. Is this true?" says Maecenas (II.ii.180-181). Pompey plays a like game with Antony, hinting at the time when Cleopatra kept an assignation with Julius Caesar by having herself rolled up inside a mattress and carried to him (II.vi.68); while Lepidus, in the brawl on Pompey's galley, speculates drunkenly—but inquiringly—about pyramises and crocodiles (II.vii.24ff.).

This is merely the surface of "report" in the play. It soon turns out that almost everyone we meet is passionately conscious of report in other senses: not simply the public report of Rome, which Caesar is concerned as far as possible to manipulate and even Antony and Cleopatra from time to time feel the need to placate or consciously defy, but the report of history. This too is an aspect of the play that insists on its aesthetic distance from us, on its character as spectacle and exemplum. Caesar is walking into history, and is keenly conscious of it; in fact, he hopes to guar-

antee a good "report" for himself by composing it: "Go with me
to my tent," he says to Agrippa and Maecenas, after Antony's
death has been announced to him:

> where you shall see
> How hardly I was drawn into this war,
> How calm and gentle I proceeded still
> In all my writings. Go with me, and see
> What I can show in this.   (V.i.73-77)

Enobarbus, throughout his hesitations about leaving Antony,
looks forward to what "story" will say of him if he stays—

> The loyalty well held to fools does make
> Our faith mere folly: yet he that can endure
> To follow with allegiance a fall'n lord,
> Does conquer him that did his master conquer
> And earns a place i' th' story.   (III.xiii.42-46)

—though it must be admitted he reckoned without Plutarch, who
gives his going over to Caesar and his repentance short shrift,
and says nothing whatever about his hesitations. Again, in his
death scene, all alone, he appeals to the "blessed moon" to bear
him witness, "When men revolted shall upon record Bear hateful
memory," that he repents his betrayal of his master, and then, as
if resigning himself to an eternity of bad notices in the *theatrum
mundi,* concludes:

> O, Antony
> Nobler than my revolt is infamous,
> Forgive me in thine own particular,
> But let the world rank me in register
> A master leaver and a fugitive.
>   (IV.ix.7ff.)

The lovers' own consciousness of being ever on parade before
the reviewing stand of world opinion is particularly acute. Antony's anguished "I have offended reputation" after Actium means
more than simply that he has stained his individual honor, or
even his immediate public image; he has also deviated from the
world's conception of what a Roman soldier is and does, guarded
and passed on from generation to generation in world opinion.
When he takes Cleopatra in his arms at the play's beginning, he
is conscious of the world as audience; in fact, he invokes it:

> The nobleness of life
> Is to do thus; when such a mutual pair
> And such a twain can do't, in which I bind,
> On pain of punishment, the world to weet
> We stand up peerless.   (I.i.36-40)

When he anticipates their reunion in the Elysian fields, he thinks of the audience they will have there:

> Where souls do couch on flowers, we'll hand in hand,
> And with our sprightly port make the ghosts gaze.
>   (IV.xiv.51-52)

When Eros takes his own life rather than kill him, the thought that captivates his imagination is that Eros and Cleopatra will have won a nobler place in history than his: "My queen and Eros/ Have by their brave instruction got upon me/ A nobleness in record."

This, too, as everyone will remember, is the concern that occupies Cleopatra as she steels herself after Antony's death to do "what's brave, what's noble...after the high Roman fashion," and so win fame, not obloquy, in the chronicles of times to come (IV.xv.8ff.). Her wish that her women "show" her "like a queen" in her "best attires" (V.ii.227-228)—though no doubt partly vanity and partly calculated staginess for Caesar's last view of her—is partly too, one feels, her sense of what is suitable, in the record that will be forthcoming, "for a princess Descended of so many royal kings." Caesar's parting words about her have the quality of an epitaph, and seal the immortality in "report" that now awaits all three:

> She shall be buried by her Antony.
> No grave upon the earth shall clip in it
> A pair so famous. High events as these
> Strike those that make them; and their story is
> No less in pity than his glory which
> Brought them to be lamented.
>   (V.ii.356-361)

Chronology of Important Dates

	Shakespeare	*The Age*
1558		Accession of Queen Elizabeth I.
1564	Shakespeare born at Stratford-upon-Avon; baptized April 26.	Marlowe born.
1572		Jonson and Donne born.
1576		Burbage builds The Theatre, the first permanent playhouse in England.
1579		North's translation of Plutarch's *Lives*.
1582	Shakespeare married to Anne Hathaway.	
1583-85	Susanna and the twins, Hamnet and Judith, born.	
1587		*The Spanish Tragedy* by Thomas Kyd. Marlowe's *Tamburlaine*, Part I.
1589		Marlowe's *Jew of Malta*.
1590		Spenser's *Faerie Queene* I-III.
1591-92	The three *Henry VI* plays; *The Comedy of Errors*.	
1592		Marlowe's *Doctor Faustus* and *Edward II*.

	Shakespeare	*The Age*
1593-94	*Venus and Adonis* and *The Rape of Lucrece* dedicated to the Earl of Southampton. *Titus Andronicus; The Taming of the Shrew; Richard III; Two Gentlemen of Verona.* Shakespeare joins in forming the Lord Chamberlain's company of actors.	Marlowe killed. Kyd dies.
1595-96	*A Midsummer Night's Dream; Richard II; Romeo and Juliet; King John; The Merchant of Venice.* The death of Hamnet.	Spenser's *Faerie Queene* IV-VI (1596).
1597-98	The two parts of *Henry IV; Much Ado about Nothing.* Shakespeare purchases New Place in Stratford.	Jonson's *Every Man in his Humour.*
1599-1600	*As You Like It; Henry V; Julius Caesar; Twelfth Night; The Merry Wives of Windsor.* Shakespeare's company moves to The Globe.	Jonson's *Every Man Out of his Humour.* Spenser dies.
1601-2	*Hamlet; All's Well that Ends Well; Troilus and Cressida.*	Jonson's *The Poetaster* (1601) and the "War of the Theaters." The abortive rebellion of the Earl of Essex.
1603-4	*Measure for Measure; Othello.* Shakespeare's company becomes the King's Men.	(1603) The death of Elizabeth and the accession of James I. Jonson's *Sejanus.*
1605-6	*Macbeth; King Lear.*	Jonson's *Volpone.*
1607-8	*Antony and Cleopatra; Timon of Athens; Coriolanus; Pericles.*	

	Shakespeare	*The Age*
1610	*Cymbeline*. The King's Men acquires the Blackfriars Playhouse.	Jonson's *Alchemist*.
1610-11	*The Winter's Tale· The Tempest*. Shakespeare retires to Stratford.	
1616	Shakespeare dies, April 23.	
1623	The First Folio edition of Shakespeare's plays.	

Notes on the Editor and Contributors

MARK ROSE, editor of this volume, is Professor of English at the University of Illinois, Urbana-Champaign. He is the author of *Shakespearean Design* and other books on Renaissance literature and is editor of *Twentieth Century Views of Science Fiction*.

JANET ADELMAN, Associate Professor of English at the University of California, Berkeley, is editor of *Twentieth Century Interpretations of King Lear*.

BERNARD BECKERMAN, Professor of Dramatic Arts, Columbia University, is the author of *Shakespeare at the Globe, 1599-1609* and other studies of drama.

REUBEN A. BROWER (1908-1975) was Cabot Professor of English, Harvard University. He was well known for books on English and American poetry, including *Alexander Pope: The Poetry of Allusion* and *The Fields of Light*.

MAURICE CHARNEY, Professor of English at Rutgers University, is the author of *Style in Hamlet* and other studies of Shakespearean drama.

JOHN F. DANBY (1911-1972) was Professor of English at the University College of North Wales and was the author of *Shakespeare's Doctrine of Nature: A Study of King Lear* and other books.

NORTHROP FRYE is University Professor of English at the University of Toronto. He has written on a wide range of literary subjects but is best known for his *Anatomy of Criticism*.

JOHN HOLLOWAY, Fellow of Queen's College and Professor of English in the University of Cambridge, has published several books of poetry as well as scholarly works on a variety of literary subjects, among them *The Victorian Sage*.

MAYNARD MACK, Sterling Professor of English, Yale University, is the author of *King Lear in Our Time* and a number of seminal essays on Shakespeare. He is also well known as a scholar of eighteenth-century literature.

JULIAN MARKELS, Professor of English, Ohio State University, has written on American literature as well as on Shakespeare.

ROBERT ORNSTEIN, Professor of English, Case-Western Reserve University, is the author of *The Moral Vision of Jacobean Tragedy and A Kingdom for a Stage: The Achievement of Shakespeare's History Plays.*

GEORGE BERNARD SHAW (1856-1950) was the author of *Caesar and Cleopatra* as well as other plays.

Selected Bibliography

Bradley, A. C., "Shakespeare's *Antony and Cleopatra*" in *Oxford Lectures on Poetry*, London, 1909. Reprinted in The Signet Edition of *Antony and Cleopatra*, ed. Barbara Everett, New York, 1964. A classic essay. Compares the play with Shakespeare's other tragedies and discusses the principal characters.

Bullough, Geoffrey, *Narrative and Dramatic Sources of Shakespeare*, vol. 5, London and New York, 1964. Reprints sources and analogues with a critical introduction.

Colie, Rosalie L., "Antony and Cleopatra: the Significance of Style" in *Shakespeare's Living Art*, Princeton, 1974. The play as a dramatization of ethical principles inherent in rhetorical styles.

Granville-Barker, Harley, *Prefaces to Shakespeare*, vol. 1, Princeton, 1946. Contains an important discussion of stagecraft, construction, and characters.

MacCallum, M. W., *Shakespeare's Roman Plays and Their Background*, London, 1910. Old-fashioned but still useful study.

Rabkin, Norman, *Shakespeare and the Common Understanding*, New York, 1967. Rabkin's approach to Shakespeare in terms of "complementarity" is particularly useful in connection with *Antony and Cleopatra*.

Ridley, M.R., ed. *The Arden Edition of Antony and Cleopatra*, London and Cambridge, Mass., 1954. Extensive annotation and a comprehensive introduction.

Schanzer, Ernest, *The Problem Plays of Shakespeare*, London, 1963. Contains a suggestive discussion of *Antony and Cleopatra*.

Spencer, T. J. B., "Shakespeare and the Elizabethan Romans," *Shakespeare Survey*, 10 (1957), 27-38. Discusses Elizabethan conceptions of the classical world.

Stewart, J. I. M., *Character and Motive in Shakespeare,* London, 1949. Contains an excellent discussion of Cleopatra.

Traversi, Derek, *Shakespeare: The Roman Plays,* Stanford, Calif., 1963. Detailed commentary on *Antony and Cleopatra.*